Ian McKinney

We hope this book
is a useful tool as
you continue to explore
the whole journey of
worship. Jackie + Nicole.

SING A NEW SONG

Choosing and Leading Praise in Today's Church

Keep singin' + shoutin'
+ strummin' that guitar.
Thanks for all the
endless hours of entertainment.
Love + Prayers
Cheryl
xo

Never stop praising Him!
Hope to hear your joyful tones
sometime soon.
hugs & kisses

"Don't you know that
I sing because I'm happy,
Don't you know that I sing
because I'm free.
His eye is on the sparrow, and I
know He watches me."
May the Lord continually rejoice
in everything you do.
Thanks for the craic!
Love + hugs
Debbie

About the Author...

David Montgomery is Associate Minister of Knock Presbyterian Church, Belfast. A graduate in English and Music from the University of Stirling, and in theology from Regent College, Vancouver, David has experience in leading worship in a wide variety of churches, large and small. He has contributed to *The Complete Book of Everyday Christianity* (IVP USA), and is on the Editorial Board of *Frontiers* magazine. David is married to Gwen and has an incurable devotion to Manchester City F.C.

SING A NEW SONG

Choosing and Leading Praise in Today's Church

David J. Montgomery

Published by Rutherford House

and Handsel Press

First published 2000
by Rutherford House, 17 Claremont Park,
Edinburgh EH6 7PJ, and Handsel Press, Millfield,
Street of Kincardine, Boat of Garten PH24 3BY, Scotland

05 04 03 02 01 00 99   7 6 5 4 3 2 1

British Library Cataloguing in Publication Data

A catalogue record for this book is available from
the British Library

ISBN 0-946068-78-X

Typeset by Rutherford House, Edinburgh
and Printed by
J. W. Arrowsmith, Bristol

In memory of John Montgomery (Senior) 1897-1994
who loved the Psalms;

and for Gwen
who knows what it is to sing a new song to the Lord.

In contrast to the joy of participating in Christian worship in the 50s, my heart sinks every Sunday when I am invited to participate in much that passes for contemporary worship — such pathetic subjective lyrics starved of theological content or even clear train of thought. I long that this book will make the churches stop and pray, before opening our mouths to sing without thinking one week longer. I will want to lay my hands on a copy and recommend it widely to others.

Michael Griffiths
Former Principal, London Bible College

CONTENTS

FOREWORD

Worship is the single most important act in which Christians engage. Some of us are convinced that it is the most significant action that takes place in the world at large, for worship repeatedly and insistently locates the centre of God's majestic rule and meaning in a world of trivial and competing sovereignties. Every act of worship promises fresh and accessible witness to God's revelation and presence. Unfortunately, not all the acts make good on the promise. All the same, 'Let us worship God' is the most important sentence spoken week after week, year after year, in congregations all over the world. It calls us to attention before God who has something life-changing, soul-saving, and world-renewing to say. It gathers us to an appropriate and adequate response to God who wills to 'make all things new', an 'all things' that includes us.

For centuries, Christians seemed to know what it meant when the call went out, 'Let us worship God...' Procedural routines and language patterns laid down in the pre-Christian centuries in Judaism were picked up and recast by the early Christians. We don't have evidence of much, if any, controversy or discussion regarding what was involved. The people of God were instructed out of a common text (the Bible), and cultivated a reliable memory, maintaining a sense of organic relationship with their ancestors (a living tradition). Worship was not exactly monolithic or predictable for variation developed through the centuries in different areas and languages; reform movements generated different styles and approaches. Still, within the various groupings, a basic consensus prevailed.

But as we enter the third millennium, there is no more consensus. When the call goes out, 'Let us worship God', instead of worshipping, men and women begin to argue, explain, advocate, promote, protest discuss, and denounce. What is spoken ranges from learned to ignorant. The rude and the courteous compete for a hearing. Not many are listening. Disorder prevails. The work of Christian worship is in chaos.

It's impossible to point the finger at anyone and assign blame—a similar chaos bedevils personal morals and world politics all across the horizon. What is possible is to go to work, beginning now, clearing away the rubble and rebuilding a life of worship adequate to the times in which we live and honouring the God whom we serve.

We find ourselves at a period in the church's life when there is a vast task of rebuilding before us on many fronts, not the least of which is rebuilding the structures and rhythms of worship that are adequate to bring us as a people before God in holy, listening obedience and robust praise. It is too early to tell exactly how this worship is going to mature. Years of careful work involving many workers in the vineyard are ahead of us.

What is important to note right now, though, is that some of these men and women, learned and devout, are hard at this work, patiently rebuilding the foundations upon which a world of Christian worship can flourish. David Montgomery is one of these. He brings a keen theological intelligence and a pastoral passion for sound worship to his work. He does not advocate a position—we really don't need more rhetoric at the moment. He works much closer to the ground; he considers and clarifies the nature of one essential element in the complex action that is worship to the glory of God, namely, the lifting of our voices in song.

Eugene H. Peterson
Emeritus Professor of Spiritual Theology
Regent College, Vancouver, B.C., Canada

PREFACE

I have written this book for a wide range of people. If your interest is in how contemporary praise fits into reformed worship, biblically and historically, then chapters 1 and 2 will be of relevance. Chapters 3 and 4 examine the poetry and music of what we sing and ask the questions: how far are good poetry and music essential to worship? Are there basic rules which lead to a song being effective? These chapters are helpful, particularly for those interested in songwriting or with responsibility for choosing praise. If your interest is in contemporary worship then chapters 5 and 6 deal with the strengths and weaknesses of some current praise music. The final three chapters consider the practicalities of leading and preparing for worship: the personnel involved, the material used, and the way in which the worship is led and presented. It is my hope and prayer that this book will be of use to traditionalist and non-traditionalist alike and that it will play a small part in encouraging all God's people to think about what they offer him as a 'sacrifice of praise' so that they may indeed worship 'in Spirit and truth'.

I have many people to thank for their help and encouragement. The Revd David Searle and Miss Lynn Quigley of Rutherford House and The Revd Jock Stein of Handsel Press read the draft and made many helpful comments, as did David Jennings (Vancouver, Canada) and Gareth Lenaghan (Belfast). I wish particularly to thank the congregations of Stormont and Knock Presbyterian Church for providing the worshipping context in which some of these ideas were conceived and nurtured, and for the countless people within those congregations and others where I have served who have discussed these issues with me, and helped to develop my thinking on this subject. Above all I wish to pay tribute to my parents who started me on the road to music and nurtured in me a love for hymns, and to my wife Gwen, who not only read the script, but without whose continual practical and spiritual encouragement (and, dare I say it, positive nagging) this book would have taken a lot longer to complete.

David J. Montgomery, Belfast, St.Patrick's Day 1999

INTRODUCTION

WHAT'S ALL THE FUSS ABOUT?

It has been said that there is no issue which divides the church more than the issue of church unity! It could equally be said that there is no greater cause of disharmony in the church than the issue of church music. Subjectivity in this area is so strong and our opinions so influenced by issues of culture, personality and taste, that what should be a secondary concern for the Christian family, often takes a central position. It is a secondary concern, for it has to do with the mere outward forms by which our primary concern—true worship of God— is expressed. Yet, when it comes to worship style, denominations are identified according to it, congregations split over it and ministers resign because of it.

For some, it is making a mountain out of a mole-hill. It is, they argue, purely a matter of taste and therefore everyone should be prepared to show tolerance for styles which they themselves do not like: this is Christian maturity and an essential component of harmonious family life.

Others disagree. They say the issue is so bound up with the theology of who we are and who God is that we cannot be flippant or careless: excellence is obligatory (and such people usually have very dogmatic views about what constitutes excellence).

Still others believe that while no dogmatic claims of superiority can necessarily be made for one style over another, it is not a case of 'anything goes'. Our worship[1] does have theological implications and we need to evaluate critically

---

[1] For the sake of convenience, and because of the topic, 'worship' in this book, unless the context clearly dictates otherwise, is used as a synonym for communal praise. I acknowledge wholeheartedly that worship is greater and broader than this, covering in fact our whole lifestyle and the totality of our experience as obedient Christians (Rom. 12:1). It is certainly not my intention to perpetuate the common misperception that worship is only about music.

exactly what we are saying to one another, to the world outside, and especially to God, when we meet together and use the God-given medium of music as a vehicle for our praise.

These various positions have tended to come into sharp focus round what has simplistically been called the 'hymn/chorus debate'. Into this debate, on both sides, come many literary and musical prejudices. It is a conflict between the old and the new, the formal and the informal, the didactic and the devotional, between 'high-brow' and 'low-brow'. It is essentially a conflict of cultures.

SAVE THE HYMN

Although this debate rages on within many congregations, it seems to me that, as far as a large section of Evangelicalism is concerned in Britain and America, the battle is over and the traditional hymn has lost! A few churches will remain dogmatically 'traditional' and resist anything contemporary, a good number more struggle to accommodate both, usually by having either a token 'hymn' or a token 'praise time' (what, we may ask, were the hymns?).

A few well-known evangelical 'flagship' congregations within mainline denominations have succeeded well in blending old and new, formal and informal, but they are a minority. Nevertheless, the fact that such mainline churches have been willing to accept philosophically and theologically the importance of balance, and have retained a good range of older material, is significant. Contrary to what is popularly thought, in terms of teaching the people of God how to worship, I believe the real work will be done in these churches, rather than in the 'new churches' which have largely abandoned traditional hymn-singing altogether.

What many in the traditional churches have not yet realised, however, is that for many believers, particularly the vast majority of those who have come to faith in the last ten years, their diet of praise is almost exclusively contemporary. This is either because their congregations sing nothing else, or because the words, images and tunes of the traditional hymns that are sung make no connection with their world, and therefore no attempt is made to learn them, remember them, or benefit from their insights.

While at theological college in Canada, for example, I was shocked that a fellow-student of several years Christian experience was totally unfamiliar with a well-known hymn I had chosen for college chapel. Similarly, a twenty-year old from my congregation in Belfast, who would have attended church weekly in addition to several contemporary youth events and college Christian Unions where he sometimes led worship, was unable to identify 'When I survey' from a CD, although he acknowledged that it was familiar, and that it sounded 'quite good'.

Nor is it fair to criticise the emerging generation of Christians for singing only what they like, or what is compatible with their musical tastes, because traditionalists are probably more guilty of this. They, after all, have been in the positions of power within the churches until recently, and have often been instrumental in excluding contemporary worship music from the services of many congregations. Furthermore, their rationale is often more illogical than that of the youth. My experience of debating these issues within several 'mainline' congregations has shown that traditionalists base their opposition to the new on a variety of prejudices ranging from volume, instrumentation, rhythm, dress-sense, repetition, modern terminology, to probably the most common (and to my mind most irrelevant) namely, the book that is used. In one church where I was leading praise there was an objection to the lack of traditional hymnody even though Luther's Reformation hymn 'A safe stronghold our God is still' had been sung, complete with archaic vocabulary. The problem was that we had sung it out of *Songs of Fellowship*![2] With the youth the prejudices tend to be simply stylistic and cultural, and this is understandable bearing in mind the cultural milieu in which they are living and their early stage of spiritual development. Elders, ministers and traditional worshippers have no such excuse and should know better. John Frame makes this point:

---

2   *Songs of Fellowship*, Kingsway: Eastbourne, 1995, no. 25.

> My observation...is that in traditionalist circles there is too much pride, too much indifference to those outside of Christ, too much wanting to be comfortable with one's own preferred styles. That too is immaturity, and worship ought to deal with it.[3]

Yet hymns are not totally foreign to those who have stopped attending church. Many will still identify correctly words from a handful of Christmas carols, hum the tunes played by the Salvation Army band, and sing along with 'Abide with Me' at the FA Cup Final. Some years ago when I was researching into Watts and Wesley, the topic would arise in casual conversation and I was surprised how familiar some of the subject-matter was to people who had stopped attending church many years ago, and how they invariably remembered the words with pleasure, like fragments of Wordsworth or Donne from school poetry books. I also remember well a couple of colleagues recounting an evangelistic conversation they had had with a prostitute who recited a well-known children's hymn verbatim and with tears in her eyes.

Equally, however, the images which hymns conjure up can be negative: memories of dreary school assemblies; fragments of archaic verse with strange words such as 'panoply', 'hobgoblin', and 'ineffable';[4] dull church services with an old organ screeching out the tune at an excruciatingly slow pace; various associations with dry, formal, soulless religion. In addition, the popular perception of the 'hymn-tune' seems to be confined to a very distinct type from the Victorian era.

---

3   J. Frame *Contemporary Worship Music*, Phillipsburg: P&R Publishing, 1997, p. 94.

4   See *Mission Praise (combined ed.)*, London: Marshall Pickering, 1990, no. 604; *The Church Hymnary, Revised Edition*, Oxford: OUP, 1927, nos. 576, 9.

Such negative associations, however valid or invalid, cannot be ignored. If there are hymns out there of good musical, literary and theological content, we need to think of ways of introducing them to modern worshippers in a context in which they will be cleansed of such negative associations and reinvested with meaning and significance. That is the challenge.

This book endeavours to do four things: firstly, to set the issue of hymn-singing within a biblical and historical context; secondly, to look at the issue of hymns as poetry and hymns as music; thirdly, to examine recent developments within hymn-writing by looking specifically at material which has emerged in the last decade; and finally, tentatively to offer suggestions for those who are faced with the task of leading congregational worship into the twenty-first century.

Chapter 1

The Biblical Context:
Psalms, Hymns and Spiritual Songs

Those who have long sought a solution to the rather
unnecessary division between 'hymn' and 'chorus/worship-
song', have tended to resort to Paul's command in Ephesians
5:19 (repeated in Col. 3:16) to 'speak to' or 'admonish one
another' in 'psalms, hymns and spiritual songs'. Here, it is
argued, is a clear three-fold level of praise outlined by the
apostle, with all levels having their proper place in the church's
worship: canonical praise (psalms), acanonical religious poetry
(hymns), and short devotional items of praise (choruses/wor-
ship songs).

This interpretation is not without its problems, not least
because it seems to be reading the text in the light of a very
specific late twentieth-century liturgical phenomenon. There
are other difficulties, however. Regarding this twice-
mentioned command, there is no immediate agreement
among scholars as to the precise differentiation of categories.
Some suggest that there may be no difference, all three
referring to freely composed improvised lyrics.[1] Some
Calvinistic churches, for example the Free Churches in
Scotland, also see this phrase as a hendiadys (a list of terms to
express one idea), but believe the terms refer to three different
sections of the canonical Psalter. With respect, although this
interpretation has a long history, it appears to be a clear case of
eisegesis (reading already held presuppositions *into* the text).

---

[1]   See C. F. D. Moule, *Worship in the New Testament*, London:
Lutterworth Press, 1961, p. 69ff.

THE REGULATIVE PRINCIPLE REVISITED

Those who favour it claim that they are adhering consistently to the 'regulative principle'. This principle, put simply, states that whatever Scripture does not command is forbidden. In over-reaction to Roman abuses in worship, the Puritans interpreted the regulative principle in such a way that everything was excluded from the worshipping environment which could not be traced back to a specific scriptural precedent. Therefore, in this scenario, unaccompanied psalms became the only valid form of sung praise. However, many within the broader reformed family have begun to question this 'restrictive, austere and minimalist' use of the regulative principle.[2]

John Frame, in particular, has contributed much in achieving an understanding of how one can maintain the regulative principle, while still admitting contemporary hymnody and instrumentation as well as movement, dance and drama in worship. Frame believes in the regulative principle. He sees this classic reformed position as stronger than the one adopted by Lutherans and Episcopalians where anything was permitted unless it was specifically forbidden, because it gives Scripture a positive and proactive authority over the whole of our lives rather than a negative reactive power of veto.[3] But for Frame, the essence of the regulative principle rests in the fact that our worship must be acceptable to God, and that we cannot simply worship 'as we please'.

When it comes to determining how that principle is applied to worship services, however, a great deal of Christian prudence is required. The Westminster Divines recognised this, and allowed flexibility in certain circumstances.[4] Frame critiques and extends their interpretation to include a wide variety of applications where flexibility and creativity are not

---

[2] J. Frame, *Worship in Spirit and Truth*, New Jersey: P&R Publishing, 1996, p. xii. I am grateful to Dr T. W. J. Morrow for his helpful comments on this book.

[3] Ibid., p. 38. For a summary of the historical arguments see J. I. Packer, *A Quest for Godliness: The Puritan Vision of the Christian Life*, Wheaton: Crossway, 1990, pp. 246-9.

[4] Westminster Confession of Faith, 1.6.

only to be permitted but are desirable: namely, the words of prayers, the accompaniment of songs, the time and place of worship services. He makes the valid point that even if one chooses to sing only Psalms, one has to choose which version, translation or metricisation to use, and whether the music will be in a traditional or modern style.[5]

Whereas the narrow Puritan application of the regulative principle was riddled with inconsistencies and prompted many fruitless debates, Frame's application is both more consistent and truly biblical. Instead of regarding some things as mere circumstances which are not bound by the regulative principle, he seeks to bring every aspect of worship (including when and where we worship) under the Lordship of Christ, so that they are honouring to God. Hence he makes no distinction between 'officially sanctioned' worship services, and 'informal fellowship gatherings', as the Puritan interpretation demands, for all worship must be as God desires. Nor does he divide worship into specific elements each of which requires a specific scriptural mandate (again as was the practice of the Puritans) for that is what typified the Old Testament tabernacle and temple, rather than the worship of the New Covenant people. Rather, he endorses the Puritans' concern for worship that is Word-based and God-honouring, but applies it more broadly. For Frame, the regulative principle more often applies to the *manner* of worship, than to its *form*.

He shows how in Scripture we find both general principles (1Cor. 10:31) as well as many relatively specific principles (Jas 2:1-4): 'Where specifics are lacking, we must apply the generalities by means of our sanctified wisdom, within the general principles of the word. Where specifics are given, we must accept them and apply them even more specifically to our own particular situations.'[6]

---

5   See J. Frame, *Contemporary Worship Music*, p. 29, n. 3.
6   Ibid., pp. 54-5.

DEFINING THE 'PSALM'

Outside of those who are enthusiastic proponents of the narrow application of the regulative principle, one struggles to find a single scholar who accepts that the three terms in Ephesians 5:19 apply exclusively to canonical psalms. It is not even clear that *psalmois* refers only to canonical psalms (see below), so any attempt to limit the scope of the other two terms is entirely without warrant. In fact, John Stott asserts that *psalmois* actually implies a musical accompaniment![7]

The language of Ephesians 5:19 and Colossians 3:16 implies some progression of thought, even if the marks of that progression are not clear. The phrase in Greek reads *psalmois humnois kai odais pneumatikais. Psalmos* occurs seven times in the NT, and in four of these it is a clear reference to the OT Book of Psalms. Of the other three, there are the Ephesians and Colossians passages, and the only other occurrence is in 1Corinthians 14:26 where Paul is discussing the components of a worship service. While consistency may suggest that *psalmos* here be translated also as 'psalm' (contra NIV 'hymn'),[8] the context implies a spontaneous revelatory song, in keeping with the other items on the list.[9]

This is further substantiated when one examines the four uses of the related verb *psallein* (Rom. 15:9; 1Cor. 14:15; Eph. 5:19 and Jas 5:13). While it cannot be proven that each verse *does not* refer to a canonical psalm, the context of all but the first makes a Christian song a more likely interpretation. N. T. Wright, in his commentary, states: 'Psalms may actually refer to the Christian use of the OT Psalter but shouldn't be restricted to that; the early church was prolific in its adaptation

---

[7] J. Stott, *God's New Society*, Leicester: IVP, 1979, p. 205. Musical accompaniment is forbidden in the free churches which rigorously follow the regulative principle.

[8] W. Bauer, *A Greek-English Lexicon of the New Testament* (2nd ed., revised by Arndt, Gingrich and Danker), London: University of Chicago Press, 1979, categorises this reference separately as 'a Christian song of praise'.

[9] See G. Fee *1st Corinthians*, NICNT Grand Rapids: Eerdmans, 1993, pp. 671, 690.

of Old Testament themes to Christian use, and in its composition of new material'.[10]

What starts to become clear as one looks at the lexical evidence, is that there is a fair amount of ambiguity and interchangeability between the terms. For example, when *humnos* (hymn) is used in Matthew 26:30 and Mark 14:26, for the song which Jesus and his disciples sang after the Last Supper, it is more than likely that this was one (or more) of the 'Hallel Psalms' (Pss 113-18) which were traditionally sung at the end of the Passover. Where the case for a narrow application of the regulative principle falls down, however, is that in 1Corinthians 14, Ephesians 5 and Colossians 3, there is contextual evidence that *not only* psalms or canonical words were being used in worship: in each case *psalmos* is part of a list.

Not only in Paul but also in Josephus[11] *psalmos* is juxtaposed with *humnos*. The other uses of *humnos* outside the specifically Jewish context of Matthew 26 and Mark 14 point to a new, creative hymnic activity which need not necessarily have a canonical base. It is used in the Septuagint for a 'new song' in Isaiah 42:10, and in Psalm 65:13 for general praise (cf. Heb. 2:12); and when Paul and Silas were in prison they rejoiced by singing *humnoi* (Acts 16:25).

THE RISE, FALL AND REBIRTH OF THE CHRISTIAN HYMN

It is true that in the 4th century there was an orthodox reaction against paraphrases replacing exact quotations of Scripture. This was probably to safeguard doctrine and is characteristic of the more controlling and hierarchical structure of authority which was emerging in the church at that time. It does however indicate that freely composed lyrics were being used. One can think immediately of the Latin classics such as the *Gloria in excelsis*, or the *Te Deum*. When Pliny the Younger wrote his famous letter regarding Christian worship he refers to the chanting of verses in honour of Christ, as to God, and

---

10   N. T. Wright, *Colossians and Philemon*, Leicester: IVP, 1993, p. 145.
11   Josephus, *Antiquities*: 12:323.

this appears to have been normative practice throughout the early centuries.[12] If one looks at Ephesians 5:18 (immediately preceding the verse discussed above), we see that this is probably a quote from an early hymn. What's more, it specifically mentions the name of Christ: 'Wake up, O sleeper, rise from the dead, and Christ will shine on you.'

In recent centuries, the person who has argued most cogently for the rightful place of hymns within the Christian church has been Isaac Watts. Famous for his hymn-writing, what is not so well-known is the fact that he had to debate rigorously for his hymns to be accepted by the church as valid for worship. Within his lifetime the majority of congregations in Britain moved from a position of singing psalms alone, to one where hymns had gained a popular acceptance: a testimony not only to the quality of his hymns but to the convincing nature of his argumentation. I have written more fully elsewhere on the arguments he employed[13] and reproduce here only a couple of his most pertinent statements:

> What need is there that I should wrap up the shining honours of my Redeemer in the dark and shadowy language of a religion that is for now forever abolished, especially when Christians are so vehemently warned in the Epistles of St. Paul against a Judaizing spirit in their worship as well as doctrine?[14]

> Moses, Deborah...David, Asaph and Habakkuk...sung their own joys and victories, their own hopes and fears and deliverances...and why must we under the gospel sing nothing else but the joys, hopes and fears, of Asaph and David? Why must Christians be forbid all other melody but what arises from the victories and deliverances of the Jews?[15]

> If the brightest genius on earth, or an angel from heaven, should translate David, and keep close to the sense and style of the inspired author, we should only obtain thereby a bright or heavenly copy of the devotions of

---

12   Pliny, *Letters* x. 96, addressed to Trajan c. AD 112. See also J. A. Smith, 'The Ancient Synagogue, the Early Church and Singing', *Music and Letters* 65 (1984), pp. 1-16.

13   'Isaac Watts and Artistic Kenosis', *Scottish Bulletin of Evangelical Theology* 5 (1987), pp. 174-84.

14   I. Watts, *Poetical Works* (7 vols), Edinburgh, 1782, vol. I, p. xxxvi.

15   Vol. I, p. xxvii.

the Jewish king, but it could never make the fittest psalmbook for a Christian people.[16]

THE PLACE OF THE 'SPIRITUAL SONG'

Leaving those who would wish to impose a rigidly canonical criterion on the categories mentioned in Ephesians 5:19, what then of those who plead for free improvisation and simple non-technical devotional repetition? Well, if they are advocating this as the *only* valid form of Christian worship, they run into similar exegetical and historical problems. The very existence of the Psalter, along with its use by Jesus and his disciples, and the existence of creative, but clearly structured early Christian hymns,[17] shows that the people of God had a canon of praise of some sort which was used repeatedly to teach doctrine and aid memorisation.

Are we then, after all, left with a threefold division which fits very nicely into the contemporary psalm-hymn-chorus phenomenon? I don't think it's as simple as that. For a start, if, as it is argued, *odais pneumatikais* refers to original, spontaneous, Spirit-given outbursts of new praise (cf. Rev. 5:9; 14:3), then virtually none of the contemporary worship choruses fall into this category. Some of these choruses are taken straight from the Scriptures, while many others tend to be written over time and tried out in different contexts, before being published and used thereafter as components in new and varied contemporary liturgies. In 1986, one of the British contemporary writers Dave Fellingham stated at a Kingsway Musicians' Conference at Swanwick that 'only once' did a song come to him immediately without any planning, experimenting or background work.

Such workshops and conferences exist to encourage *and teach* song-writing within this medium. No, it appears that contemporary choruses must be judged *by the same criteria* as

---

16   Vol. I, p. xliv.
17   See above. It is inconclusive, but still possible, that some NT passages such as Phil. 2:6-11, or 2Tim. 2:11-13 were hymns or fragments of hymns. For arguments against see G. Fee, *Philippians*, NICNT, Grand Rapids: Eerdmans, 1995.

traditional hymns, for there are no exegetical or theological reasons to regard them as being in substance different. The spiritual songs to which Paul alluded probably were, or at least included, spontaneous charismatic praise offerings.[18]

THE ROLE OF THE 'HYMN'

How then should these acanonical hymns/songs be defined? One of the earliest standard definitions was by Augustine who defined a hymn as containing the three elements of 'song', 'praise' and 'towards God'.[19] This, however, could discount the possibility that hymns may not only be 'to God about God' ('Immortal, invisible, God only wise'); or 'to God about us' ('My faith looks up to thee'); but also 'to us about God' ('Onward Christian soldiers').[20] This dimension of mutual encouragement is clearly expressed in both the Colossians and Ephesians passages. While both do mention that the praise is directed towards the Lord, both also contain the command to speak to, or admonish *one another*. Such a horizontal dimension can also be seen in certain of the psalms.[21]

It appears that, when considering the lyrics of hymns, several factors need to be held in tension such as biblical faithfulness, congregational edification, and poetic competence.

The fact that a piece is poetically and musically excellent is not sufficient to warrant its inclusion in worship if it teaches theology which is antithetical to Scripture. If hymns, as I argue later, have a didactic role to play, bad theology is counter-productive and inappropriate for the context of worship. I am certainly not advocating, of course, an avoidance of such works of music or literature, nor saying that Christians can only be edified by reading that with which they agree. Rather, that in the very specific context of worship, truth is of the utmost

---

18 G. D. Fee, *God's Empowering Presence*, Peabody: Hendrickson, 1994, pp. 653-4, 885-6.

19 See A. Wilson-Dickson, *The Story of Christian Music*, Oxford: Lion, 1992, p. 25.

20 *Mission Praise*, nos. 327, 469, 543.

21 E.g. Pss 95, 122.

importance (John 4:24) and the exclusion of material on this basis is valid.

Congregational edification is also important. Rogal distinguishes, for example, between the hymn and other types of religious poetry. Some offerings from poets such as Donne and Emerson ('Hymne to Christ'; 'Concord Hymn') may technically qualify as hymns but their contribution to corporate worship would probably be minimal.[22]

Neither should one forget the role of good poetry. For example, if the work is not poetically disciplined, but crowded with images, colloquialisms, bad use of metre or rhyme, or anachronistic terms which grate on the ear, it becomes a hindrance rather than an aid to worship. Dean comments:

> A hymn is one of the most tightly structured poems in the tradition....
> Few poets these days have learned the skill of writing such formal verse....
> To speak naturally about God, one's emotions, and one's ultimate
> concern in tight restrictive poems is not something modern or post-
> modern poets do well.[23]

So, to return to Paul, it seems that, with the exception of a spontaneous charismatic outburst of joy (which is an entirely different matter), and use of the canonical Psalms, all other material must fall under the category of *humnoi*, and be analysed accordingly. But this should not imply restriction to one type of *humnos*. In all of this, the key word is variety. Tom Wright reminds us: 'Together these three terms indicate a variety and richness of Christian singing which should neither be stereotyped into one mould nor restricted simply to weekly public worship.'[24]

---

22 S. J. Rogal, *A General Introduction to Hymnody and Congregational Song*, Metuchen: Scarecrow, 1991, p. 6.

23 W. Dean, *A Survey of Twentieth Century Church Music in America*, Nashville: Broadman Press, 1988, p. 223.

24 N. T. Wright, *Colossians and Philemon*, p. 145.

Chapter 2

The Historical Context:
Knowing our Roots

PRE-20TH CENTURY

Although there are more than a few pre-Reformation compositions in all contemporary hymn-books from writers such as Theodulph of Orleans, Bernard of Clairveaux, Thomas Aquinas, Bianco da Siena,[1] it would be wrong to think of these as hymns composed for the same purposes for which modern hymns are composed.[2]

The genesis of the English hymn as we know it, really lies with Isaac Watts. Once Watts succeeded in getting hymns accepted by the churches of his day, the floodgates opened and the next two centuries were ones of prolific hymn-writing. Wesley, Newton, Cowper and Montgomery stand at the head of an army of lesser names, many of whose work has been forgotten, but some of whom will be immortalised by one or two 'greats'. For example 'Crown him with many crowns', 'The God of Abraham praise', and 'All hail the power of Jesus' name', are the only notable survivors from the pens of Matthew Bridges, Thomas Olivers and Edward Perronet, respectively.[3] It is also important to realise that the texts as we

---

[1] See *The Church Hymnary, Third Edition*, Oxford: OUP, 1973, nos. 233, 377, 584, 115.

[2] Routley writes: 'Whenever [these older hymns] are so used [in modern worship] they are adaptations of old material to a use for which it was not originally designed, in response to a demand of which the mediaeval liturgists were not conscious.' E. Routley, *Christian Hymns Observed*, Princeton: Prestige, 1982, p. 12.

[3] See *Mission Praise*, nos. 109, 645, 13.

have them now have often gone through revisions. This was happening in Germany from the end of the 18th Century and became an accepted practice elsewhere. As Wilson-Dickson pertinently comments: 'Perhaps those who baulk at present-day revisions would do well to consider how many changes their favourite hymns may already have suffered before reaching the pages of a modern hymn-book.'[4] Feder also remarks:

> There always had been some change, but rewriting of texts on a large scale was characteristic of the second half of the 18th century.... People objected to the irregular metric structure of the old hymns, to the impure rhymes, to the liberties taken with word order, to the partial unintelligibility, to certain expressions felt to be uncouth or ambiguous, to a typical early Protestant mood of belligerence, and, in Pietistic hymns, to the spiritual eroticism.[5]

Musically, the standard psalm tune was supplemented with a rather folksy, sometimes florid, 'Methodist tune' employed by the Wesleyans as a more suitable accompaniment for the new hymnody that was emerging from their Movement. It was a key element in their methodology that these tunes should be attractive and singable to everyone, not just an elite group of musical literates, although not everyone was accepting of this, particularly in establishment circles. It was not until the 20th century that the 'establishment' book *Hymns Ancient and Modern* (first pub. 1861) contained the popular Helmsley to Wesley's 'Lo! He comes with clouds descending'. The lyrical dance-like style of the tune was for many years regarded as inappropriate for the words.[6]

Nineteenth-century sacred music was characterised by three developments: the 'Victorian' hymn-tune (for example, Barnby's O Perfect Love and Dykes's Nicaea 'Holy, holy, holy');[7] cathedral music in the style of Stainer, Attwood and

---

4   Wilson-Dickson, op. cit., p. 111.
5   G. Feder, in F. Blume (ed.), *Protestant Church Music: A History*, New York: Norton, 1974, pp. 336-7.
6   See E. Routley, *Twentieth Century Church Music*, London: Herbert Jenkins, 1964, pp. 197-8; and W. Shaw, in Blume, op. cit., p. 727.
7   *Mission Praise*, nos. 517, 237.

Maunder; and the emerging Gospel song (exemplified by Sankey and Bliss). This era also saw an increase in musical literacy (through the tonic sol-fa system), and the introduction of Novello's cheap octavo editions. Hymns from different sources were collected into books, so that households as well as congregations had regular access to the hymns of the period.

Significantly, what we find is that a disproportionate amount of this material survives over a century later. This could be due to a number of factors. For instance, the compositions of previous centuries had been filtered and reduced to the few classics contained within the hymn-books of this period. Further, since this was the first era when music could be published for the people and bought and read by the people, there is an expected concentration of contemporary pieces. But most significantly of all perhaps, the subsequent musical conservatism of the church meant that later compositions which did not conform to the expected form and structure of the 'Victorian' hymn struggled to gain acceptance. The main hymnological event of this century was the publication of *Hymns Ancient and Modern* and a major by-product of this hymnal was the way in which certain hymns were married to specific tunes in the public consciousness, perhaps forever. Hymns, previously as diverse and idiosyncratic as the authors who wrote them, were in danger of being stuck forever in nineteenth-century garb.

20TH-CENTURY TRADITIONAL HYMNODY

In 1899 Robert Bridges published his *Yattendon Hymnal*. It was characterised by his very artistic translations of many older Latin or German hymns,[8] but this literary renaissance was not to be followed by later twentieth-century hymnographers. Instead, the new Evangelical hymn writers, such as Dudley-Smith, Perry and Idle, pursued a modern but simple articulation of doctrinal fundamentals, especially in their

---

8   E.g. 'All my hope on God is founded', *The Church Hymnary, Third Edition*, Oxford: OUP, 1973, No. 405.

Christmas and Easter hymns.[9] Although writers such as Fred Kaan occasionally addressed modern issues of urbanisation, civil rights, war and peace, it is his sacramental hymns which have gained widest acceptance.[10] The task of addressing contemporary issues in hymnody has been resumed by John Bell and Graham Maule, and these will be looked at in detail in chapter 6.

Musically, out of the late-nineteenth century in England came outstanding composers such as Stanford and Parry who wrote mainly for choir, but left a couple of good hymn tunes, such as Engelberg ('For all the love') and Repton ('Dear Lord and Father of Mankind').[11] Vaughan Williams with his major contribution to the English Hymnal of 1906 introduced an important English folk-music strand to hymnody seen, for example, in the setting of Forest Green to 'O little town of Bethlehem'.

Twentieth-century hymnody, both lyrically and musically, displays a reaction against Victorian sentimentalities. Martin Shaw's tunes, such as Little Cornard ('Hills of the North, Rejoice'),[12] are characterised by unison sections and harmonies that are 'broadly diatonic and sometimes touched with modalism'.[13] Dean highlights the key elements of a twentieth-century tune as: rhythm, climax, word-appropriateness, range and melodic movement, mood and colour.[14] However these technical and literary-style hymns have not proved popular or been accepted willingly by generally conservative congregations. This has been a factor in the general lack of enthusiasm which greeted the hymnbook still used in the majority of Scottish and Irish Presbyterian churches, *The Church Hymnary, Third Edition*, which contains a number of these tunes.[15]

---

9   All of these authors are well represented in *Hymns for Today's Church*, Hodder: London, 1982.
10 See *Hymns for Today's Church*, nos. 414, 419.
11 *Hymns for Today's Church*, nos. 204, 356.
12 *Hymns for Today's Church*, no. 242.
13 W. Shaw, in Blume, op. cit., p. 728.
14 Op. cit., p. 225.
15 See nos. 141, 148, 411.

Similarly, with the compositions of David Peacock and John Barnard who, between them, have 46 tunes in *Hymns for Today's Church* (1982), it is noteworthy that very few of these have proved to be singable by the average congregation. Tunes from recent decades which have proved more popular include Beaumont's Gracias ('Now thank we all our God'), and Chesterton ('Lord thy word abideth'); Baughen's Majestas ('Name of all majesty'), and Brierley's Camberwell ('At the name of Jesus').[16]

POPULAR HYMNODY

The popular stream of hymnody was represented in earlier years by publications such as Sunday School song books, mission-hall hymnals and youth-orientated collections. But as Wilson-Dickson correctly observes 'there has been a consistent time lag between a musical fashion in the secular world and its adoption by Christian music'. Scripture Union choruses reflected music-hall tastes, and *Youth Praise* (1966) 'betrayed the musical interests of its adult compilers and bore little relation to the secular youth music of the time'.[17] This is a problem that is still with us.[18]

Although the conflict between old and new, formal and informal may seem to be more marked in our generation, it has been with us before. Dean outlines the rationale behind the conflict which arose between the 'establishment' and the aficionados of the gospel-song at the turn of the century:

> In general, the musicians and the theologians joined forces to keep the gospel songs out of the denominational hymnals, and sharp controversies arose in their attempts to define and categorise 'hymns' and 'gospel songs'. These attempts were based upon their literary value, theological content, and musical style characteristics. The gospel song was derided by many as being no more than doggerel verse, written by amateurs with little poetic skill. The texts were also attacked as being sentimental, egocentric, having crude poetic imagery, and little foundation in biblical

---

16 *Hymns for Today's Church*, nos. 33(ii), 251(ii), 218(ii), 172(i).
17 Wilson-Dickson, op. cit., pp. 240-41.
18 See my comments on the style of current songwriters such as Redman, in chapter 5 below.

theology. Further, they argued, the gospel song was not addressed to God, but was an interpersonal message of testimony. A basic element of worship was thus bypassed, making such songs unfit for corporate worship.[19]

While some of these criticisms are difficult to counter, not all of them are valid. While music has many functions within a worship service, its missiological potential cannot be forgotten. If the church is to be effective in mission, there is a need for music which is immediately accessible to the people, and which can communicate the truths of the Gospel in a recognisable idiom. Similarly, the charge of subjectivity ignores the fact that many of the biblical psalms were written in the first-person and entirely subjective. Routley comments that looking through collections of gospel songs 'is to be confronted by page after page of music all in a single style'[20] but, he rightly observes, this is no different from leafing through some of the transient specialised hymnals of the previous century. Sunday Schools, temperance and mission organisations all had their own 'gospel-song books' reflecting a taste and style which has now passed into oblivion. This was simply the popular music of the era, and it in turn would be replaced by later pieces of equally transient value.

RENEWAL MUSIC AND THE CONTEMPORARY SCENE

An interesting development has taken place in that more recent compilations of contemporary worship songs such as *Spring Harvest Worship*, and *Mission Praise* have increased their tally of older hymns, and have a general worship theme rather than the evangelistic and 'invitation' pieces which characterised collections such as *Alexander's Hymns*.[21] On the other hand, Dean observes, 'the Billy Graham crusades have brought universality and a degree of permanence to many

---

19 Dean, op. cit., p. 91.
20 E. Routley, *Christian Hymns Observed*, p. 82.
21 E.g. 'Almost Persuaded', or 'Throw out the lifeline' *Alexander's Hymns No.3*, London: Marshall, Morgan & Scott, n.d., nos. 107, 94.

gospel songs' such as 'Blessed Assurance', 'The Old Rugged Cross' and 'Trust and Obey'.[22]

Charismatic and renewal music has evolved from the early 1970s with Karen Lafferty's 'Seek ye first'[23] commonly regarded as the progenitor. One of the features of this evolution is the way in which songs, initially at least, have emerged from among the grass-roots of the movement. This was seen first in publications from the Fisherfolk in the U.S.,[24] and then in the *Songs of Fellowship* series from Kingsway Publishers in Britain. Prominent writers however have emerged: Owens, Howard, Paris, plus more recently the Vineyard corps in the US; Kendrick, Bilborough, Fellingham, Bowater and now Richards, Smith and Redman in Britain. One wonders how long the grass-roots element will be significantly represented in publications to come.

Stylistically, this type of music was preempted by that emerging from the community at Taizé in France. Wilson-Dickson summarises the characteristics of this movement as 'short musical phrases with singable melodic units that could be readily memorised by everybody,'[25] but, whereas Taizé's music was basically liturgical and Latin, the renewal songs in England and America covered the full range of unfettered personal devotion. The dividing line between classic hymn-form and devotional chorus is often clear-cut, but sometimes blurred (as in early Kendrick, for example). Like the gospel-song, these pieces exhibit a simple melody, basic and predictable harmony, and a rather unsubtle use of musical climax. However, they are less metrical, and the words tend to consist either of the repetition of a single devotional phrase ('Sing Hallelujah to the Lord'), or a straightforward setting of scriptural text ('Seek ye first'; 'I am the bread of Life').[26] An interesting divergence from both this 'charismatic' stream and the 'classical hymnody' of Dudley-Smith et al., can be seen in

---

22 Dean, op. cit., p. 83. See *Mission Praise*, nos. 59, 536, 760.
23 *Mission Praise*, no. 590.
24 *Sounds of Living Water*, 1974, *Fresh Sounds*, 1976, *Cry Hosanna!*, 1980.
25 Wilson-Dickson, op. cit., p. 227.
26 See *Mission Praise*, nos. 601, 590, 261.

the songs of the Iona Community in Scotland, who have built on the Celtic folk tradition; but more of that later.

It is impossible not to generalise about such a wide variety of material, but, in fairness, it should be pointed out that clear stylistic differences have emerged within this genre. The Fisherfolk sound of the 70s is not the Kendrick sound of the 80s, and neither of these is the Vineyard or Spring Harvest sound of the 90s. It is undeniable that much renewal music has matured, becoming harmonically more interesting, technically more demanding, and rhythmically more varied, and it appears that the popular church music of today is becoming as wide and as varied as the contemporary heterogeneous pop culture.

Chapter 3

Getting the Ingredients Right:
Words that Inspire

There are those who would question the extent to which we should analyse hymns. Does it matter whether a piece is good poetry or not? To what extent is the quality of music relevant, so long as people are helped to worship? While few would deny that the best hymns are also good poetry,[1] Isaac Watts deliberately repressed his poetic skills in order to communicate. 'High-brow' enthusiasts who believe the more literary hymns to be superior, simply because of their poetic complexity, over against simple devotional choruses, would do well to remember that the purposes of literature and worship are not the same, and to heed Watts's own words. In the Preface to his hymns he writes of his motivation: 'I would neither indulge any bold metaphors, nor admit of hard words, nor tempt an ignorant worshipper to sing without his understanding.'[2]

Neither Watts nor Wesley believed that the hymn was fully-fledged poetry. Hymns by their nature are open to a constant revision of words and settings, have only limited use apart from their function as an aid to praise and, as a vehicle for the emotions, should not be seen as an end in themselves. Too many ambiguities, obscure references or lofty images distract the worshippers' attention from the task in hand. Yet such restrictions need not be stifling. They can challenge and inspire

---

[1]   See R. Manwaring, *A Study of Hymn-writing and Hymn-singing in the Christian Church:* Lewiston: Edwin Mellen Press, 1990, p. ix.

[2]   *Poetical Works*, vol. I., p. xlii.

the author to search for new and interesting ways of expressing old truths within the limitations of the hymn-form.

Equally, just as overtly flowery language can be off-putting, so too is unpolished doggerel. Anyone who has to use the Scottish metrical Psalter regularly will know only too well how inaccessible it has become to late twentieth-century ears, and how the passion and power of the original has been disguised with the convoluted syntax of such lines as 'I joy'd when "to the house of God, go up," they said to me' and: 'Thy way to God commit, him trust; it bring to pass shall he'.[3]

HYMNS AS POETRY

There is therefore an important role for good poetry in hymnody and if Christian poets would apply their gifts to this needy area it would be to the great benefit of the wider church. This is particularly important when one bears in mind the extent to which contemporary poetry has drifted from its Christian roots. What then makes for good poetry in a hymn? Space permits only a brief mention of some guiding principles. These are, to an extent, arbitrary and, like many 'rules' in the arts, not without important exceptions. They will not be noticed in good hymns, for good hymns draw our minds to the theme, not the form; bad hymns, on the other hand, will usually have failed in one or more of these areas.

Structure

To sing the work of an author who has crafted his or her product, developing the themes, utilising contrast and imagery, careful repetition and interesting vocabulary, is a much more rewarding experience than singing something which has been 'thrown together' to fit a catchy melody. A very simple example is 'Low in the grave he lay'.[4] The writer views the resurrection from three different angles. There is Christ himself in verse 1; the religious and political authorities

---

3   *The Psalter, Revised edition*, Oxford: OUP, 1899, Pss 122:1 and 37:5.
4   *Mission Praise*, no. 453.

in verse 2 ('Vainly they watch his bed'); and the powers of evil in verse 3 ('Death cannot keep his prey'); all within a very simple 'call and response' structure. This is not a development so much as three different 'shots' of the same scene, but it works. There is a fine progression of thought in 'Lord, I lift your name on high', which is all the more disciplined because of the piece's brevity. The second half runs like this:

> You came from heaven to earth to show the way,
> From the earth to the cross, my debt to pay,
> From the cross to the grave, from the grave to the skies,
> Lord I lift your name on high.[5]

On the whole, however, many contemporary pieces show no sign of compositional forethought, and instead are examples of what I call a 'cut-and-paste' approach; a compositional collage. One recent song, unpublished (I hope), which I heard in North America, contained the verse:

> In your house are many mansions,
> At your gate you feed the poor,
> Blessed are the poor in spirit,
> For they shall be made new.

Nothing essentially wrong with each individual line, but the progression is more 'stream of consciousness' than development of a theme.

Rhyme

Rhyme has never been an essential component in hymnody. Ambrose never felt obliged to make his hymns rhyme, and the Scottish Psalter is evidence enough that having rhyme can be a liability as much as an asset. Similarly in the popular, and otherwise great, 'All hail the power', the need to finish each verse with 'all', has led to some cumbersome endings such as 'this terrestrial ball'.[6]

---

5 SH97, no. 85.

6 *Mission Praise*, no. 13. See *Hymns for Today's Church*, no. 203, for a reasonable, if rather severe revision.

The much more limited use of rhyme in the 'rock' medium has meant that contemporary ears do not expect it so quickly, or notice its absence as much as those of a previous generation. At a recent youth event, for example, I found only three rhymes on the entire song-sheet. This is not necessarily a bad thing, but one must be careful that the removal of this 'obligation' is not seen as an excuse for lazy composition.[7] Nor must we forget that rhyme greatly assists memorisation, and that a song's lifespan will depend to an extent on whether it is easily remembered (or worth remembering).

Sometimes the rhyme can be subtly embedded in the verse, in half-lines, or by following a different pattern to the usual 'a-b-a-b', 'a-b-c-b' sequences. In the examples below the pattern is 'a-b-b-a' and 'a-a-b-c-c-b'.

> O who am I, that for my sake,
> My Lord should take frail flesh and die?
>
> ...But, O my friend, my friend indeed,
> Who, at my need, his life did spend.[8]
>
> The Lord gives eyesight to the blind;
> The Lord supports the fainting mind;
> He sends the labouring conscience peace:
> He helps the stranger in distress,
> The widow and the fatherless,
> And grants the prisoner sweet release.[9]

The first of these is by the Puritan Samuel Crossman, the second by Watts. These traditional hymns certainly have a freshness which is due in part to the different rhyming sequence employed.

In Fred Kaan's wonderful reflection on the Magnificat, the verses are written in couplets but, since this can get tiresome in repeated verses, in the third stanza the rhyme is underplayed

---

7   I am reminded of a cartoon I once saw of a worshipper singing from 'The Happy Clappy Songbook' a piece which ran: 'We praise thee for our fellow man, / who sings to you as best he can, / his psalmody may rhyme and scan, / but sometimes it doesn't!'

8   From 'My song is love unknown', *Mission Praise*, no. 478.

9   From 'I'll praise my maker while I've breath' *Mission Praise*, no. 320.

by linking lines two and three in a single clause:

> By him, the poor are lifted up;
> He satisfies, with bread and cup,
> The hungry folk of many lands;
> The rich must go with empty hands.[10]

While this can be an effective poetic device, the tune to which this is sung must be chosen carefully. A tune with too long a break at the end of line two will lead to the meaning of this verse being lost.

Some more modern hymns have departed even further from traditional rhyming expectations. In many ways it is harder to write a quality song which is rhymeless but still exhibits the marks of careful craftsmanship. Saward's 'These are the facts' makes no attempt at rhyme but is still firmly within the traditional hymn genre, and is carefully crafted. Its tight metre and climax of vocabulary beginning with the basis of our preaching, climbing through the fulfilment of Scripture and the indwelling of the Spirit, to the climax of the eternal hope of the believer, illustrate the author's very deliberate formation of the song.

> These are the facts as we have received them,
> These are the truths that the Christian believes,
> This is the basis of all of our preaching:
> Christ died for sinners and rose from the tomb.
>
> ...Christ has fulfilled what the Scriptures foretold,
> Adam's whole family in death had been sleeping,
> Christ through his rising restores us to life.
>
> ...We, with our Saviour, have died on the cross;
> Now, having risen, our Jesus lives in us,
> Gives us his Spirit and makes us his home.
>
> ...We shall be changed in the blink of an eye,
> Trumpets shall sound as we face life immortal
> This is the victory through Jesus our Lord.[11]

---

10   *Songs of God's People*, Oxford: OUP, 1988, no. 96.

11   *Hymns for Today's Church*, no. 162.

This popular rendition of Psalm 124 by Christopher Idle is another good non-rhymng example:

> This earth belongs to God,
> The world, its wealth and all its people;
> He formed the waters wide
> And fashioned every sea and shore.
>
> Who may go up the hill of the Lord
> And stand in the place of holiness?
> Only the one whose heart is pure,
> Whose hands and lips are clean.[12]

Kendrick's 'We Believe' is an excellent example of a creative use of rhyme.

> We believe in God the Father, Maker of the Universe,
> And in Christ, his Son, our Saviour, come to us by virgin birth;
> We believe he died to save us, bore our sins, was crucified,
> Then from death, he rose victorious, ascended to the Father's side....
>
> We believe he sends his Spirit, on his church with gifts of power,
> God, his Word of truth affirming, sends us to the nations now;
> He will come again in glory, judge the living and the dead:
> Every knee shall bow before him, then must every tongue confess....[13]

Here there is only one full rhyme, but the others are half-rhymes or 'vowel-rhymes', which are fiendishly difficult to employ well. It is often much easier to force a full-rhyme, but in so doing not communicate as precisely. Stuart Townend's excellent piece, 'How deep the Father's love', makes good use of weak rhyme:

> Behold the man upon a cross, my sin upon his shoulders;
> Ashamed, I hear my mocking voice call out among the scoffers.
> It was my sin that held him there until it was accomplished;
> His dying breath has brought me life, I know that it is finished.[14]

---

12 *Let's Praise*, London: Harper Collins, 1994, no. 208.
13 *Mission Praise*, no. 720.
14 SH98, no. 51.

A good rhyme doesn't draw attention to itself, but assists in exposing the meaning of the words. One of the faults of the 'gospel-song' was that it really had only one theme, and therefore the interest in the successive verses was how this theme could be fitted into different rhyming patterns. Hence we see an over-abundance of lines ending with 'me... tree... Calva<u>ry</u>', 'died... crucified... supplied' etc.

The contemporary song has not shed some of these shortcomings.[15] Take the second verse of 'As the Deer', for instance, where the author's choice of first line ending threw up a real challenge for line three:

> I want you more than gold or silver
> Only you can satisfy,
> You alone are the real joy-giver,
> And the apple of my eye.[16]

Here there is no real progression of thought, and a careless use of a biblical image. God's people are said to be the apple of his eye (Deut. 32:10; Ps. 17:8; Zech. 2:8) and we are told to keep *his teachings* as the apple of our eye (Prov. 7:2), but this verse has reduced the biblical figure of speech to one of weak sentimentality.

Repetition

One of the frequent complaints against the new repertoire is its repetitiveness. But repetition can be used creatively. Note the well-known first verse of 'And can it be':

> *And can it be* that I should gain
> An interest in the saviour's blood?
> Died he *for me who* caused his pain,
> *For me who* him to death pursued?
> Amazing love! *How can it be*
> That thou my God, shouldst die *for me*?[17]

---

15   Indeed 'He's Given His All', SH98, no. 43, is a good example of formulaic terminology and very predictable rhyme.

16   *Mission Praise*, no. 37.

17   *Mission Praise*, no. 33.

Or the three-fold 'great' in 'To God be the Glory' :

> *Great* things he hath taught us, *Great* things he hath done,
> And *great* our rejoicing through Jesus the Son.
> But purer, and higher, and *greater* will be
> Our wonder, our rapture, when Jesus we see.[18]

Similarly, we see it in Watts's classic stanza:

> See from *his* head, *his* hands, *his* feet,
> *Sorrow and love* flow mingled down;
> Did e'er such *love and sorrow* meet,
> Or thorns compose so rich a crown?[19]

and in Wesley's famous carol:

> Mild he lays his glory by,
> *Born* that man no more may die,
> *Born* to raise the sons of earth,
> *Born* to give them second birth.[20]

However, this is not a case of 'the old' getting it right, and 'the new' failing. Some older hymns are guilty of poor repetition:

---

[18] *Mission Praise*, no. 708.

[19] *Mission Praise*, no. 755. Repetition can be particularly effective if used within the confines of a single line, as in 'All blessing and all blest' ('Hail to the Lord's anointed', *Mission Praise*, no. 204), and 'Seven whole days, not one in seven' ('King of Glory', *Mission Praise*, no. 397).

[20] *Mission Praise*, no. 211. This verse is also an excellent example of Wesley's biblicism. Each line can be traced to a direct scriptural quote or at least a biblical principle:

Hail, thou heaven-born Prince of Peace,	Isa. 9:6
Hail, thou Sun of Righteousness.	Mal. 4:2
Light and life to all he brings,	John 1:4,9
Risen with healing in his wings.	Mal. 4:2
Mild he lays his glory by,	Phil. 2:6,7
Born that man no more may die,	1John 4:9
Born to raise the sons of earth,	Eph. 2:1, 5
Born to give them second birth.	John 3:3

In his struggle to get hymns accepted as biblical worship, Isaac Watts also claimed 'I might have brought some text or other and applied it to the margin of every verse' (*Poetic Works*, vol. 3, p. xiii.)

> Break thou the bread of life,
> To me, to me.[21]

Neither are all repetitions in contemporary worship songs inappropriate or ineffective: the repetition of 'be to our God for ever and ever' in 'Salvation belongs to our God'[22] is natural. The theme of the song is everlasting praise, and the words are complemented by the music and the rhythm. Nevertheless, the majority of repetitions in recent songs are not as appositely linked to the theme or the music, and many could justifiably fall under Christ's rebuke of being 'vain' (Matt. 7:6).

Furthermore, when some hymnbook compilers print 'etc.' at the bottom of pieces, they really have abdicated their role as providers of quality material and shapers of worship, and have simply mirrored a contemporary cultural trend to 'Do-it-Yourself'. There is a place for improvisation in music and even in lyrics within the worship service, but by definition this cannot be planned, or written into a hymnal. Sometimes this tendency becomes ridiculously illogical. How, for example, can 'the greatest thing in all my life' be 'knowing you' *and* 'loving you', *and* 'serving you' *etc.*! [23]

Imagery

Evocative imagery and careful scene-setting can be so effective in bringing alive a biblical event. See how Kendrick, with an economy of words, beautifully captures the desolation of the *via dolorosa*, in 'Come and See':

> Soldiers mock, rulers sneer
> As he lifts the cruel cross;
> Lone and friendless now
> He climbs towards the hill.[24]

---

21   *Mission Praise*, no. 64.
22   SH97, no. 114.
23   Matt. 7:6. (*Mission Praise*, no. 646).
24   SH97, no. 20.

Two of the older hymn-writers, George Matheson and Samuel Johnson, have colourfully painted pictures of, on the one hand, dying and rising with Christ; and, on the other, the believer's eternal security in a hostile world.

> I lay in dust life's glory dead
> And from the ground there blossoms red,
> Life that shall endless be.
>
> In vain, the surge's angry shock,
> In vain the drifting sands:
> Unharmed upon the eternal Rock
> The eternal city stands.[25]

When one is aware of Matheson's tragic blindness, his use of colour in this hymn, along with words such as 'light', 'flickering torch', 'sunshine's blaze' and 'rainbow' are all the more poignant.

In contrast to the pastoral and rural images which dominate traditional hymns, Kaan is one of the few who roots his hymns in the urban world:

> He calls us to revolt and fight
> With him, for what is just and right
> To sing and live 'Magnificat'
> In crowded street and council flat.[26]

Similarly Wren's harvest hymn has proved popular in urban congregations struggling to find ways of celebrating a rural festival:

> Praise God for the harvest that's sent from afar,
> From market and harbour, from tropical shore:
> Foods packed and transported, and planted and grown
> By God-given neighbours, unseen and unknown.

---

25 From 'O Love that wilt not let me go', *Mission Praise*, no. 515; and 'City of God', *The Church Hymnary, Third Edition*, no. 422.

26 I have been unable to track down the bibliographical reference for this hymn which does not seem to have appeared in more recent hymnals.

> Praise God for the harvest that comes from the ground,
> By drill or by mineshaft, by opencast mound;
> For oil and for iron, for tinplate and coal,
> Praise God, who in love has provided them all.[27]

Among the modern crop of writers, in spite of the rapid urbanisation of the world, and the fact that these writers live and work in urban contexts, many still lazily overuse rural images of mountains and rivers in their worship songs. One exception would be 'As Sure as Gold is Precious'. Although I criticise it below for its too bland 'revival-speak', Robin Mark has done an excellent job in painting some word-pictures of urban life:

> As sure as gold is precious and the honey sweet,
> So you love this city and you love these streets.
> Every child out playing by their own front door;
> Every baby laying on the bedroom floor...
> Every dreamer dreaming in her dead-end job;
> Every driver driving through the rush hour mob.[28]

Metaphors and Similes

Metaphors are to be found in countless numbers of hymns and praise songs, old and new, many of them borrowed directly from Scripture:

> Christ is made the sure foundation,
> Christ the *head and cornerstone*.
> Chosen of the Lord, and precious,
> Binding all the church in one.[29]

> *Rock* of Ages, cleft for me,
> Let me hide myself in thee.[30]

> Crown him with many crowns
> The *Lamb* upon the throne.[31]

---

[27] From 'Praise God for the harvest', *Hymns for Today's Church*, no. 288.
[28] SH98, no. 8.
[29] *Mission Praise*, no. 73.
[30] *Mission Praise*, no. 582.
[31] *Mission Praise*, no. 109.

Bread of heaven, Bread of heaven,
Feed me till my want is o'er.[32]

You are my *Rock*, in times of trouble,
You lift me up when I fall down.
All through the storm,
Your love is the *anchor*.[33]

Timothy Dudley-Smith's hymn 'As water to the thirsty' is entirely constructed around a succession of similes:

Like calm in place of clamour,
Like peace that follows pain,
Like meeting after parting,
Like sunshine after rain;
Like moonlight and starlight
And sunlight on the sea,
So is my Lord,
My living Lord,
So is my Lord to me.[34]

Alliteration

Alliteration, when used sparingly can make an otherwise ordinary line lodge in the mind. See how Henry Lyte takes Isaiah 40:6-7 and the concept of the transience of life, in 'Praise, my soul':

Frail as summer's flower we flourish.[35]

A few other selected examples are listed below:

Led like a lamb to the slaughter
In silence and shame.[36]

My Captain leads me forth,
To conquest and a crown.[37]

---

32   From 'Guide me, O thou great Jehovah', *Mission Praise*, no. 201.
33   From 'Faithful One', SH98, no. 23.
34   *Hymns for Today's Church*, no. 470.
35   *Mission Praise*, no. 560.
36   *Mission Praise*, no. 402.
37   From 'Join all the glorious names', *Mission Praise*, no. 392.

Unresting, unhasting, and silent as light
Nor wanting, nor wasting, thou rulest in might.[38]

Strong Deliverer, Strong Deliverer,
Be thou still my strength and shield.[39]

Alliteration is best employed when it doesn't draw attention to
itself, but simply aids the flow of the lyric. In the two
examples below, the alliteration is not at first obvious:

O Lord, dark powers are poised to flood
Our streets with hate and fear
We must awaken!
O Lord, let love reclaim the lives
That sin would sweep away
And let your kingdom come.[40]

We have a hope that is steadfast and certain,
Gone through the curtain and touching the throne;
We have a Priest who is there interceding
Pouring his grace on our lives day by day.[41]

On closer examination, one can see, in the first example, that
the choice of some of the words such as 'poised' and 'sweep
away' has been carefully made. Other words could have been
used, but these heighten the poetic effect, and raise the lyric
above the ordinary. (Notice too, how this is achieved without
employing any rhyme). In the second example, the alliteration
is more subtle still: the word 'certain' is linked to what has
gone before through the 's' and soft 'c', and to what comes
after through its rhyme with 'curtain'. The word 'touching'
has been carefully chosen over other equally valid words such
as 'reaching', and there is also a perceptible aural connection
between the words 'priest' and 'interceding'.

While very little of the above analysis will be obvious to
the first-time (or even the regular) worshipper, it doesn't need

---

38 From 'Immortal, invisible, God only wise', *Mission Praise*, no. 327.
39 From 'Guide me, O thou great Jehovah', *Mission Praise*, no. 201.
40 From 'O Lord, the clouds are gathering', *Mission Praise*, no. 509.
41 From 'Jesus is King', *Mission Praise*, no. 366. A super contemporary
    hymn, but for the superfluous 'do' in the final verse.

to be. What matters is that, by taking a little more care over the crafting of their material, the writers of these relatively contemporary songs have ensured, by the sounds and rhythms of the lyrics they have used, that the words are easier to recall and therefore the songs stand a greater chance of being used for years to come.

Contrast

A simple but effective use of contrast can be seen in the song 'Give thanks':

> And now, let the weak say 'I am strong',
> Let the poor say 'I am rich'.[42]

Kendrick's 'Come and see', once again, is a worthy example, with its contrasts at the beginning of the final verse:

> Man of heaven, born to earth,
> To restore us to your heaven. [43]

Theme

In chapter 5 I comment on how some contemporary collections are limited in their use of theme. On the more serious level this betrays a theological imbalance, but it is also evidence, on the literary level, of a lack of creativity. Since God is Sovereign over all of life we could benefit from some bold experiments in hymns that express this sovereignty over such macro–issues as sport, commerce, travel, and politics. I wrote the following to assist Irish churches reflect on the post-1998 Irish Peace Process:

> Land of conflict, tears and trouble,
> Twisted truth and love suppressed;
> Hoping for a fearless future,
> Searching for a trustful rest.
> God, who once the great peace process
> Through the Great Peace Envoy planned,

---

[42] *Mission Praise*, no. 170.
[43] SH97, no. 20

By your peace-fruit planting Spirit,
Bring your peace to heart and land.

Land of beatings, blasts and bullets,
Loving evil, hating good;
Land where anger, pride and half-truth
Poison speech and attitude.
At the cross two forms of justice,
Earth's and heaven's, together stand,
God of justice, truth and mercy,
Bring your justice to our land.

Land of doubt, distress, division,
Fractured families, feuding friends;
Land where cynical suspicion
Stifles all that good intends.
Barrier-breaking, curtain-rending
God of Gentile and of Jew,
Reconcile us to each other,
Reconcile us all to you. [44]

There is also a dearth of hymns that name, and place within a theological context, some of the personal issues, big and small, with which many of us struggle. Problems such as family break-ups, redundancy, childlessness, failure, debt, or use of time. The issue of time may not seem to be an obvious, or even appropriate theme for a hymn, but how many Christians struggle, not only with their stewardship of time, but with living with an appropriate perspective on the past and the future? Fred Kaan bravely tackles this theme. His hymn begins:

Thank you, O Lord, for the time that is now;
For all the newness your minutes allow.

It then deals with the past:

Thank you, O Lord, for the time that is past,
For all the values and thoughts that will last;

---

[44] 'Land of conflict', *A Time to Heal: the church as a community of peace, justice and reconciliation*, Belfast: ECONI, 1998.

May we all stagnant tradition ignore,
Leaving behind things that matter no more.

The next verse deals with the future, but notice the clever link between the final phrase of this verse and the opening one of the next:

Thank you for hopes of the day that will come,
For all the change that will happen in time (*half-rhyme*)
Lord, for the future, our spirits prepare,
Hallow our doubts and redeem us from fear.

Make us afraid of the thoughts that delay,
Faithful in all the affairs of today
Keep us, O Father, from playing it safe,
Thank you that now is the time of our life! [45]

With that final half-rhyme, Kaan has not only brought the hymn to a suitable climax, but has concluded the theme magnificently by utilising and transforming a well-known cliché to act as an inspiration to faithful Christian living in the here and now.

REVISING AND UPDATING

What needs to be borne in mind throughout these analyses is that the worst of the old has passed into oblivion and what we are comparing is the best of the past with the, as yet, unsifted contemporary repertoire. It is also important to remember that some of the failings mentioned above still exist in older songs. Furthermore, the use of archaic words and phrases such as 'which wert and art', in 'Holy, holy, holy'[46] is liable to shorten its life-span unless revisions like that of Jubilate Hymns ('you were and are') achieve widespread acceptance.

Linguistic updating has always been a feature of hymnody. Well-known hymns such as 'When I survey the wondrous cross', 'Hark the herald angels sing', and 'Lo! He comes with clouds descending', have already been revised from what

---

45   *Partners in Praise*, Great Yarmouth: Galliard, 1979, no. 150.
46   *Mission Praise*, no. 237; *Hymns for Today's Church*, no. 7.

Watts, Wesley and Cennick originally published. Even a publication as conservative as the Presbyterian Metrical Psalter acknowledges in its preface the need for some revision:

> As it is now more than two hundred years since the admirable Scottish Version was prepared, several of its words and phrases and not a few of its grammatical forms, have become antiquated; while through the progress of Hebrew scholarship and the labours of critical expositors, some of its renderings have been shown to be inaccurate.

> In the present Revised Version an attempt has been made to remove these blemishes by emendations of those portions where there are erroneous renderings, errors of syntax, faulty rhymes, obsolete words, or want of correspondence between the rhythm of sense and the rhythm of sound.[47]

The tragedy is, of course, that over a century has passed since the revisers began their work, and their version which they imagined would hold good for a generation or so, has achieved a sacrosanct status in many Scottish and Irish churches to this day.

In the realm of hymnody, Jubilate Hymns are the compilers of *Hymns for Today's Church*, and several other publications, and their updating of the language in hymns, while bound to anger traditionalists, is absolutely necessary if these hymns are to be saved from oblivion. Compare the following:

Wesley	*Jubilate Hymns*
Long my imprisoned spirit lay,	Long my imprisoned spirit lay,
Fast bound in sin and nature's night:	Fast bound in sin and nature's night:
Thine eye diffused a quickening ray,	Your sunrise turned that night to day,
I woke—the dungeon flamed with light.	I woke—the dungeon flamed with light.[48]

---

47   *The Psalter, Revised edition*, p. v.

48   Cf. *Hymns for Today's Church*, nos. 588, 452. The compilers recognised that this hymn, and six others, were so popular that changing them would evoke considerable opposition. Even in their first edition, therefore, they printed a revised version and then the traditional one in

As with all Bible translations, the results will not be uniformly good in everyone's eyes. In 'Praise to the Lord, the Almighty', for example, 'Shelters thee under his wings' has been replaced with 'keeping us safe at his side'.[49] While this is a reasonably accurate 'dynamic equivalent', the original phrase is still comprehensible, and the revision loses the connection with the image which is so common in the Old Testament, particularly the Psalms.[50] Nevertheless, what is gained through these alterations in terms of intelligibility, far outweighs whatever shortcomings may be evident in individual revisions. Churches which readily accept contemporary translations of the Word of God, have no reason to object to the updating of the poetry of men and women.

POETRY TO STRETCH THE MIND AND MOVE THE HEART

The contemporary preference for informal and loosely structured pieces diminishes their memorability and, I believe, their long-term value. Charles Wesley said he wanted to use the 'purity, strength and elegance of the English language' in his writing.[51] Until there are more like-minded writers composing for today's church, we may have to continue looking back to find the best words with which to praise our God.

The Wesleys also saw their hymns as a vital didactic tool, and we do well to remember that these were written not for a population where third-level education was the norm, but often for illiterate people who were nevertheless able to grasp

---

an appendix. The other six were: 'Praise God from whom all blessings flow', 'All hail the power of Jesus' name', 'Come, Holy Ghost, our souls inspire', 'He who would valiant be', 'The Lord's my Shepherd', and the National Anthem. When the time arrived for the second edition (1987) these had been supplemented with 'Rock of ages', 'Holy, holy, holy', 'Lead us, Heavenly Father, lead us', 'O Thou who camest from above', and 'O Come all ye faithful'.

49 Cf. *Mission Praise*, no. 564 and *Hymns for Today's Church*, no. 40.
50 See Ruth 2:12; 1Chr. 28:18; 2Chr. 5:8; Pss 17:8; 36:7; 57:1; 61:4; 91:4.
51 Qtd. R. Manwaring, op. cit., p. x.

fundamental doctrines such as conversion, penitence, justification, sanctification and glorification as expounded in Charles's hymns. In spite of the passage of centuries, few have matched the succinctness with which Wesley captures the joy and triumph of the resurrection in such lines as 'Vain the stone, the watch, the seal; Christ has burst the gates of hell.'[52] Kendrick comes as close as any modern hymnwriter in these magnificent verses:

> Hell had spent its fury on him,
> Left him crucified.
> Yet by blood he boldly conquered,
> Sin and death defied.
>
> Now the fear of death is broken,
> Love has won the crown.
> Prisoners of the darkness, listen,
> Walls are tumbling down.[53]

Whether one chooses the traditional or revised words of 'And can it be?' (see above), Wesley's description of the liberation of conversion in the rest of that verse is surely unmatched:

> Long my imprisoned spirit lay,
> Fast-bound in sin and nature's night....
> My chains fell off, my heart was free,
> I rose, went forth, and followed thee.[54]

We badly need twenty-first-century songwriters of comparable theological insight and poetic skill.

Since the role of hymnody is to assist both the mind and heart to worship, the use of appropriate words is vital, and the music must at all times be a servant to the lyrics. This will be an increasingly difficult discipline to enforce in a post-modern culture where, in the popular media, and even in certain areas of education, text is becoming subordinated to music and image.

---

52 From 'Christ the Lord is risen today', *Mission Praise*, no. 76.
53 From 'In the tomb so cold', *Mission Praise*, no. 340.
54 *Mission Praise*, no. 33.

One modern author, who had experience writing for multimedia encyclopaedias, and other CD-Rom based educational tools, explained his frustration:

> My disillusionment with multimedia grew less out of any principled objection than from a slow accretion of insults and revelations.... There were the routine demonstrations of text's low rank on the CD-Rom totem-pole: whenever software engineers had trouble cramming all the visual components on to a disc, we writers would simply be told to chop our texts in half.[55]

Our culture is becoming increasingly de-verbalised, and this has profound theological implications. As people's active vocabulary diminishes, and inter-generational communication becomes more and more difficult because each new generation adopts its own exclusive slang and terminology, Babel is revisited, and the gospel is undermined. Language is an important part of our humanity as created in the image of the God who speaks. Fragmented and broken linguistic frameworks are signs of a broken and fragmented humanity, unable to communicate with God or with each other.

In the later chapters we shall see how, in many of the latest contemporary worship-songs, the lyrics are almost incidental, and probably deliberately so, with words and phrases (often clichés) chosen for their sound rather than their meaning. It appears that many contemporary writers of worship material have accepted the deverbalisation of the culture uncritically, and do not see their role being that of providers of good quality lyrics. The fact that many current songwriters and worship-leaders are first and foremost musicians goes some way to explaining the dual phenomena of the popular appeal of their songs, and the general weakness of many of the words.

This is not a revisitation of tired old arguments by an unreconstructed traditionalist, but a plea to recognise the importance of words *in worship*. One of the commonest criticisms of rock music, for example, by previous generations,

---

55   P. Roberts: 'The Future of Writing', *Independent on Sunday: Sunday Review*, 29 September 1996, pp. 11-14.

was 'we can't hear the words'. Such criticism betrayed a lack of understanding regarding musical form. In some rock music the words were meant to be incidental, the vocal line acting like another instrument. The same effect can be seen, of course, in the vocal melismas of many classical choral works, including sacred oratorios. But we are dealing here with communal worship, and hymnwriters have an obligation to ensure that the people of God are edified by what they sing.

Chapter 4

Getting the Ingredients Right:
Music that Moves

THE IMPORTANCE OF THE MUSIC

Donald Webster, lecturer and choirmaster in Edinburgh for many years, has written that 'it is the tune which rightly or wrongly has the primary appeal where hymns are concerned, and this becomes evident when people are invited to choose their favourite hymns.'[1] This is a reality, albeit an unfortunate one. No tune, however good, should excuse the inclusion of a hymn which may be unorthodox, vague, or empty of theological content. [2]

Nevertheless, the importance of the tune cannot be ignored. Many a good hymn has been lost because it has become attached to a dreary or unsingable tune. Take Robert Murray McCheyne's exquisite poem for example:

> When this passing world is done,
> When has sunk yon glaring sun,
> When we stand with Christ in glory,
> Looking o'er life's finished story,
>   Then, Lord, shall I fully know,
>   Not till then, how much I owe.[3]

---

1   D. Webster, *Our Hymn Tunes: Their choice and performance*, Edinburgh: Saint Andrew Press, 1983, p. ix.

2   For a banal humanism see 'The Family of Man' by K. F. Dallas, *Partners in Praise* (from the Methodist Church Division of Education and Youth), no. 149; and no. 92, 'Life is great' by Brian Wren, which is not really redeemed by the last verse. Fortunately these seem to have been sifted out of later collections.

3   *The Church Hymnary, Revised Edition*, no. 582.

The poignant lyrics of this and subsequent verses have struck a chord with virtually all who have come across it, and yet it is very rarely sung. Although it appeared in *The Church Hymnary, Revised Edition*, it was dropped from the third edition and does not appear in any more contemporary hymnals. I have heard a couple of locally written tunes which serve it well for individual congregations, but for immediate universal use, try it to *Lowliness*, the tune normally associated with 'Who is he, in yonder stall?'[4]

Hymnbook compilers have struggled long with this issue, knowing that many hymns can be 'married for life' to the tunes to which they were set in major hymnals.[5] To see how a hymn can be given a whole new perspective through a change of tune try 'How sweet the name of Jesus sounds' to the exquisite Bowater/Tredinnick tune *Rachel*, instead of the bland *St Peter*;[6] or 'What a friend we have in Jesus' to the contemplative Welsh tune *Ebenezer* ('Oh the deep, deep love of Jesus'), rather than the jaunty *Converse*.[7]

Given the servant nature of the music, and yet the imperative that the tunes must be appealing if the hymn is to be sung at all, what are the criteria of a good tune? If the search for objective literary criteria was hard, the musical quest is arguably harder. Opinions on this matter can easily be dismissed on the basis of 'subjective taste', and whenever anyone attempts an authoritative list of criteria counter-claims and contradictions abound.

William Reynolds cites one churchman's criteria for evaluating hymn tunes.[8] This gentleman compiled a list of around a dozen characteristics of superior and inferior hymn-tunes. Unfortunately it begs the question 'superior in whose eyes?' Thus 'predominant use of basic note values in the

---

4   As set in *The Church Hymnary, Revised Edition*, no. 77; *The Church Hymnary, Third Edition*, no. 221.

5   See comments on *Hymns Ancient and Modern*, in chapter 2 above, and on *Darwall* in n. 52 below.

6   *Hymns for Today's Church*, nos. 211(ii) and (i).

7   As set in *The Church Hymnary, Revised Edition*, no. 701, (i) and (ii).

8   W. Reynolds, *Survey of Christian Hymnody*, New York: Holt, Reinhart & Winston, 1963, pp. 131–3.

melody' and 'two or three changes (of harmony) per measure', are signs of superior tunes, while 'typical waltz rhythm' and 'echo-type melodies' are traits of inferior tunes. What appears to be happening here is that the author is looking at tunes he likes, distinguishing them from those he doesn't like and making the differentiating criteria into a litmus test by which to judge all music. This is just not adequate.

Even Donald Webster's analyses, while technically correct, can still betray his own subjective preferences, and even prejudices. He has a general tendency to use loaded phrases such as 'second-rate and second-hand' (re., for example, 'The Old Rugged Cross').[9] He refers to worshippers who are 'materially, culturally and spiritually deprived' as opposed to the 'thinking agnostic'.[10] Other unsubstantiated criticisms of tunes are couched in words such as 'tawdry accompaniment', 'Philistinism', and 'monstrosities'[11] while *Lyngham* 'exudes a certain extrovert vulgarity'.[12] Beaumont's tunes are described variously as 'superficial', 'corny', 'ephemera', 'in defiance of musical fitness', 'gimmicks' and 'cliché-ridden'[13] and his rendering of 'O Jesus, I have promised' is damned with faint praise by being referred to as 'catchy in a superficial sort of way'.[14] Webster's singling out of Geoffrey Beaumont for criticism throughout the book is both unnecessary and unjustified. In the end the criticisms are so weak in content that they say more about Webster's musical prejudices than about Beaumont's music. Undeniably, his comment that 'if one lives constantly in a worshipping atmosphere of fine hymn tunes, one instinctively spots the shoddy and rejects it'[15] has a degree of truth in it, but is still not very helpful in bringing us closer to defining what is 'fine' or 'shoddy'.

The Archbishops' report did not take us any further in this regard either, stating: 'It is of some comfort to recognise that

---

9   Op. cit., p. 2.
10   Ibid., p. 9.
11   Ibid., pp. 9, 16, 22.
12   Ibid., p. 29.
13   Ibid., p. 100.
14   Ibid., p. 19.
15   Op. cit., p. 36.

often that which is really good stands out just as clearly as that which is of poor quality'.[16] It goes on to say:

> In the end the choice is best based not on personal preferences but on asking the question, 'Within the style which is suitable, comprehensible and helpful to my congregation, is this piece of the best quality that I can find?' [17]

A good question to ask, and not a bad rule of thumb, but I'm not sure that that is even the final arbiter. Besides, the report continues with the sentence 'The answer to that question may not always be easy'. In fact, John Frame exposes the inadequacy of using quality as the only criterion:

> We might say, for the sake of argument, that 'A Mighty Fortress' is the best hymn ever written. Then singing anything else would involve a decrease in quality. The conclusion, then, would be that we should never sing anything other than 'A Mighty Fortress', because any other hymn would be less than 'the best'. Then the best way of planning worship would be to find the best hymn(s) ever written and sing them over and over again.[18]

It should be obvious that this would be ridiculous. The reality is that there are a large combination of factors which will justifiably determine the most appropriate choice of praise, such as a need to refrain from singing the same few songs repeatedly, or a need to achieve a balance of style or mood in the service as a whole. Frame recognises this:

> There are...times and situations where quality as an abstract concept must and should be overridden by other considerations. The fact that hymn A is musically and textually superior to hymn B doesn't imply that we must always prefer A over B. The worship literature abounds in exhortations to bring before God 'only the best'. I have declared...my agreement with that basic idea. But we should not place an absurdly literal interpretation on the word 'best'. In this context, best simply means music that is *generally excellent* and *adequate for its purpose*.[19]

---

16 *In Tune with Heaven: The Report of the Archbishops' Commission on Church Music*, London: Hodder & Stoughton, 1992, para. 166.
17 Ibid., para 167.
18 J. Frame, *Contemporary Worship Music*, p. 108.
19 Ibid., p. 108, italics mine.

Musical Rules

As in literature, there are generally accepted 'rules' of musical language which, when adhered to, enable the music to communicate as effectively as any spoken language. If the rules are broken indiscriminately the music fails to perform its appropriate function as a servant of the words. Nevertheless, the rules can occasionally be 'stretched' or momentarily abandoned: in a discord, an unexpected melodic jump, or change of time or key. In fact it is these exceptions which transform a moderate tune into a great tune. Otherwise all worship music would be left sounding like examples from a music theory primer.

Paramount, of course, is a tune's singability. A piece of music may be technically brilliant, but if it is unsingable to the average worshipper, it loses all value as a hymn-tune. William Booth, who abolished choirs and any music that the people could not appreciate, once defined a 'good tune' thus:

> A melody with some distinct air in it, that one can take hold of, which people can learn, nay which makes them learn it, which takes hold of them and goes on humming in the mind.... That is the sort of tune to help you; it will preach to you and bring you believers and converts.[20]

This aside, common traits in well-received tunes include: matching musical phrases and sequences, unexpected 'catch-phrases' or motifs, creative use of rhythm, appropriate climaxes, use of harmony or accompaniment, and the suitability of the tune to the words.

Imitation of Musical Sequences

This is such a fundamental aspect of melodic writing that it is impossible to give more than a few examples.

---

[20]   Wilson-Dickson, op. cit., p. 139.

E.g. 1 *Praise my soul* ('Praise, my soul, the king of heaven')[21]

E.g. 2 *Lasst uns erfruen* ('All creatures of our God and King')[22]

E.g. 3 *Nativity* ('Come, let us join')[23]

E.g. 4 'Give thanks with a grateful heart'[24]

In *Nativity* and *Praise, my soul*, the phrases are an integral part of the fabric of the whole tune, whereas in the majority of contemporary pieces everyone is aware of and expects the repetition. Although there are many poor examples of this,[25] it doesn't have to be done badly. In 'Give Thanks' the imitation flows with the rhythm of the words and the melody changes

---

21   *Mission Praise*, no. 560.
22   *Mission Praise*, no. 7. This piece is actually based on a series of five consecutive repeated phrases.
23   *Mission Praise*, no. 93.
24   *Mission Praise*, no. 170.
25   See *Mission Praise*, no. 133, 'Father, I place into your hands', for a clear example of tedious musical repetition.

sufficiently in the middle section to prevent the phrase from becoming tiresome.

In contrast, many of the melodic lines in contemporary worship songs are negatively repetitive and undeveloped. The songs of Martin Smith, for example, could be described as musically impressionistic. The main purpose of the music is to create an atmosphere through repeated chords, steady rhythm, and a single melodic motif, or sometimes two: one for the verse and one for the chorus.

E.g. 5 'Did you feel the mountains Tremble?'[26]

This motif is repeated with only slight variation a tiresome eight consecutive times before making way for another equally repeated phrase. Aside from its lyrical vacuousness (see below), the gaps, rhythm and melodic range of this piece make it impossible to sing corporately. A reasonably competent band may be able to make this sound interesting through creative accompaniment, but this is not, by any stretch of the imagination, a congregational song, particularly with so many high F-sharps!

---

[26]   SH97, no. 25. The same compositional technique can be seen in his 'History Maker' (SH98, no. 70), and 'It's Rising Up' co-written with Redman (SH98, no. 71).

E.g. 6 'Over the mountain and the sea'[27]

O - ver the moun - tain and the sea, Your ri - ver runs with love for me,

Chorus

I could sing of your love for e - ver,

Here Smith is content with one major motif for the verse, and another for the chorus. It could be argued that the lyrics 'I could sing of your love forever' naturally lend themselves to repetition,[28] which would be fine if the song was simply sung once or twice. However, I have yet to be in a service where this piece was played, and where I didn't get the impression that the worship leader was taking Smith's sentiments literally!

Another Spring Harvest song 'Heavenly Father' by Mizen and Pressdee,[29] is totally impressionistic with various melodic sequences sung recitative-like over a bass E which remains constant for the whole piece.

Kevin Prosch's 'He is the Lord'[30] is another example of one motif for the verse and one motif for the chorus. Bearing in mind the number of times these songs tend to be repeated in many services, it is virtually impossible to keep the mind active and engaged during worship. These songs appear to be contributing to a major 'dumbing-down' of worship, whereby mental activity is openly discouraged in preference for 'heart-worship'. Matt Redman has named Prosch as one of his major influencers,[31] and certainly Redman's songs and performances exhibit the same impressionistic repetition. At the end of one of his best songs 'I will offer up my life,' we have the totally

---

27   SH97, no. 106.
28   See ch. 3, n. 22 above.
29   SH98, no. 47.
30   SH98, no. 41.
31   From the Worship Together website at:
    www.gospelcom.net/worshiptogether/previous/mattredman.html

unnecessary riff 'What can I give, what can I bring?'; and he repeats this in 'Can a nation be changed?'[32]

There are of course good and creative melodies in among the collection. Redman's 'Once Again'[33] is simple but effective and well-developed, while the Richards's 'Hold Me Closer'[34] is infuriatingly catchy and whistle-able, in the best traditions of pop. Mark's 'As Gold is Precious', and Kendrick's 'No Scenes of Stately Majesty'[35] make good use of the pentatonic scale which underlies most folk music. The former is rhythmic and up-beat with longer than expected, but not difficult, breaks between the lines; the latter more reflective and mellow.

Rhythmic Variety

The traditional hymn form is certainly not renowned for this. Yet, in very subtle ways, differences can be inserted by the composer which transform otherwise unexceptional tunes. Note the anticipated penultimate note in the line reproduced in the example below.

E.g. 7 *Vulpius* ('The Strife is o'er')[36]

Example 8 is a particularly good illustration of rhythmic versatility. Here, in contrast to the steady opening sequences of notes, the middle section contains the almost staccato 'Jehovah, Great I AM', giving way to the flowing half-beats of 'by earth and heaven confessed'.

---

32 SH97, nos. 65,17.
33 SH98, no. 72.
34 SH98, no. 49.
35 SH98, nos. 8, 102.
36 *Hymns for Today's Church*, no. 163 (ii).

E.g. 8 *Leoni* ('The God of Abraham praise')[37]

Je - ho - vah,   Great   I   AM,   By   earth   and   heaven   con - fessed

Among more contemporary pieces, 'There is a Redeemer', and 'Brother, sister, let me serve you', have very straightforward and unambitious tunes, both of which are saved from ordinariness by a slight change in the last line. In example 9 it is the short melisma on 'Holy', and in example 10, the change to 3/4 time for a single bar.

E.g. 9 'There is a Redeemer'[38]

Pre - cious Lamb of   God,   Mes- si - ah,   Ho-   ly   One.

E.g. 10 'Brother, sister, let me serve you'[39]

let   you   be   my   ser -   vant   too.

Smith's 'What a Friend I've Found'[40] actually changes from 4/4 to 5/4 for the penultimate bar, while Baker's 'The Father's Heart is Breaking'[41] concludes with an unexpected triplet on the decisive words 'send me'. In Redman's 'I will offer up my life', the unexpected lengthening on the word 'part', is a beautiful touch, which gives a sense of climax to the tune and

37   *Mission Praise*, no. 645.
38   *Mission Praise*, no. 673.
39   *Irish Church Praise*, Oxford: OUP, 1990, no. 99. Also known as 'Brother, let me be your servant'.
40   SH98, no. 149.
41   SH98, no. 126.

is also well-suited to the words, providing a thoughtful pause after the phrase 'O my words could not tell'.

E.g. 11 'I will offer up my life'[42]

Oh my words could not tell,   not e-ven in part,   of the debt of love that is owed

Rhythm is the dominant feature of most contemporary music, yet modern worship songs do not always develop this to its full potential, preferring to 'play safe', exhibiting a little more flexibility than the traditional genre, but still having nothing really new to offer.

An exception would be some of the material from the Vineyard Fellowships. Their earlier material was not particularly innovatory, and concentrated more on being devotional, characterised by haunting melodies, and longer than usual line-breaks, as in 'It's your blood that cleanses me'. But in later volumes there are some interesting varieties: reggae 'It is the cry of my heart',[43] gospel 'Let us rejoice in the Lord', and rock 'Father of Lights'. The last of these along with others such as 'Holy is the Lord', depends for effect entirely on the ability and improvisation of the accompanying musicians. The songs themselves are sparse to say the least—two lines of words ('Father of lights') or five notes ('Holy is the Lord'). Here we are sitting at the frontier between what is possible, or even productive, for the average congregation to learn, and what should be left to performers. In the last two cases mentioned I think we have crossed the boundary, but a piece such as 'I will give thanks' has sufficient content and a good flow, so as to be manageable by at least some groups.[44]

---

[42] SH97, nos. 65.
[43] *Let's Praise*, no. 323.
[44] For these examples and others, see *Worship: Songs of the Vineyard*, Anaheim: Vineyard, vols 1-3, 1991; vol. 4, 1993. 'It's your blood' can be found in a simplified form in *Mission Praise*, no. 351.

Some of these more band-orientated pieces have found their way into mainstream collections. Let's Praise, for example, includes some complex pieces, from well-known Christian performers, and other songs with pages of additional instrumentation. While Adrian Snell's 'We your people' is easily adaptable for congregatonal use, as is Amy Grant's 'Your word is a lamp', Michael Card's 'I have decided' and the songs of Bill Batstone are probably still best suited for performance.[45]

A striking difference between contemporary worship songs and traditional hymnody would be the presence of long rests in between lines. These are usually filled with guitar or keyboard motifs, as in example 12, and require a strong lead from the musicians or else congregations will be left floundering.

E.g. 12 'Don't let my love grow cold'[46]

The comment must be made at this point that many who favour the contemporary pieces often don't fare any better in coping with long line breaks, nor is the congregational singing necessarily better in, for example, charismatic worship services. The differences between the latter and the average traditional congregation are to do with context and mindset. With a full band playing and singers and musicians being well amplified, the volume from the congregation is low and sometimes inaudible, therefore 'wrong entries' or 'missed beats' tend to go unnoticed. Besides, an 'atmosphere' has been created where the worshippers' minds have been diverted from the detail of

---

45   *Let's Praise*, nos. 219, 232, 76, 75.
46   SH97, no. 26; see also 'His banner over me' no. 42 and many other Vineyard songs mentioned above.

the music, and the focus is at least on the relaxing 'mood' of the songs and (hopefully) on the God about whom they are singing. This is not the case when one attempts to introduce such songs with a minimal guitar accompaniment into a traditional context—perhaps a service in a spacious church with good vocal acoustics. Here slip-ups in timing are obvious and create discomfort, adding to any existing prejudices against the new music.

While, in the former case, the concentration on God rather than on the intricacies of musical performance is to be welcomed, concern could be expressed at the way in which the domination of the leading band deprives the worshippers of the experience of participating in communal worship, and they could easily, in some cases, be reduced to the role of spectators.

Another very common characteristic in contemporary worship music is the regular anticipation of the first beat, and an emphasis on the 'off' beat, in, for example, the chorus of 'Rejoice, Rejoice'.

E.g. 13 'Rejoice! Rejoice!'[47]

Re - joice!   Re - joice!   Christ   is   in   you

This type of syncopation is probably the single greatest factor separating the 'old' from the 'new'. Those brought up on a diet of 'Old 100th' and 'Aurelia'[48] find such pieces hard to play and frustrating to sing. Of course, on the other hand, it is the mono-rhythmic nature of many traditional hymns which makes them less appealing to the modern ear. Kendrick's 'My heart is full'[49] is a well-written song based on Hebrews 1, but is probably most memorable for the complete break in the accompaniment for half a beat before a syncopated rising motif

---

47   *Mission Praise*, no. 572.
48   *Mission Praise*, nos. 20, 126.
49   SH98, no. 97.

introduces the climactic words 'All the glory, honour and power belong to you'.

Musical Climax

In both traditional and contemporary hymns, musical climax can play an important part in bringing a tune to life. It is often employed to match words such as 'Hallelujah' (examples 14 & 17), or 'Rejoice' (example 15), and, in each of these cases, to accompany words which remain the same in each verse of a piece, even when the piece doesn't officially have a refrain as such (examples 16 & 17).

E.g. 14 *Victory* ('The strife is o'er')[50]

Here a totally unremarkable series of musical sequences (very loosely adapted from Palestrina) is saved from being tedious by a simple 'Hallelujah', and as a result, this piece has become a most appropriate Easter hymn. It becomes even more effective if it is sung creatively, using various groups within the congregation to sing different verses, with all joining in on the final shout of praise.

E.g. 15 *Darwall* ('Rejoice the Lord is King')[51]

---

50   *Hymns for Today's Church*, no. 163 (i).
51   *The Church Hymnary, Revised Edition*, no. 135 (i), where it is set to this hymn. Alternatively, *Mission Praise*, no. 783.

In this instance the climactic 'Rejoice', with which each verse ends, is anticipated by a simple ascending scale. The sense of climax is heightened by the fact that the scale bridges the normal lining of words and music. Therefore, although the breaks would be expected to follow pattern A, they actually follow pattern B. This gives the hymn a sense of anticipation through the mini-climax at the words 'heart' and 'hear', and then a greater triumphant finish at the end of each verse.

Pattern A	*Pattern B*
Lift up your heart, lift up your voice,	Lift up your heart
Rejoice, again I say, 'rejoice!'	Lift up your voice, rejoice, again
	I say 'rejoice!'
We soon shall hear th'archangel's voice	We soon shall hear
The trump of God shall sound, rejoice!	Th'archangel's voice, the trump of God
	Shall sound, rejoice!

This is also an excellent example of a superb marriage of tune and words, since neither hymn nor tune were written for each other. *Darwall* is more correctly called *Darwall's 148th*, after the psalm it was composed to accompany; and Handel's *Gopsal* was the tune originally written for Wesley's words.[52]

E.g. 16 'Restore, O Lord'[53]

men may see and come with rev-erent fear to the Li-ving God

Like *Darwall* this climax is anticipated by a scale. Here the chromaticism draws it out a little more, and then the climax arrives, not at the end, but cleverly on the penultimate line with the words 'Living God', and with a little syncopation for

---

52   See *Mission Praise 1*, London: Marshall, Morgan & Scott, 1983, no. 195, where the tune is strangely called *Handel*. It is a curious fact that although *Darwall* is associated with these words in many circles, most hymnbooks, including *Mission Praise* no. 575, only print *Gopsal* for this hymn.

53   *Mission Praise* no. 579.

added effect. Each verse ends with a different theme: the eternal reign, mercy and presence of the living God. But the musical emphasis is where it should be: on the divine name.

E.g. 17 *Daylight* ('Darkness is gone')[54]

pro - mise to do a new thing   is   done, and Hal - le - lu - jah,

Again, this climax doesn't come at the end of the piece, but in the part of the hymn where the writer switches from what has been achieved in the resurrection, to our response. The link word in the penultimate line of each verse is 'Hallelujah', and the majesty of the words is aided by the tune reverting to stately longer beats after a couple of matching lines with a half-beat motif.[55]

The following two songs are discussed below in relation to good use of harmony, but they also serve to illustrate well a good sense of musical climax.

E.g. 18 *Lamb of God*[56]

still free - ly flow - ing, still cleans - ing, still heal -ing,   I ex - alt   you

Up to this point, the tune, which began with simple semi-staccato three-note phrases to accompany the tri-syllabic phrases 'Lamb of God, Holy One, Jesus Christ, Son of God, lifted up, willingly...', has developed by means of parallel four-note sequences before the long D on 'Healing' gives a sense of anticipation resolved by the appropriate words 'I exalt you'.

54   *Enemy of Apathy*, Glasgow: Wild Goose Publications, 1990, p. 70.
55   See also 'Lord I come to you' SH98, no. 87 discussed in the next chapter.
56   SH98, no. 83.

In 'Jesus shall take the highest honour' there is an intermediate climax, introduced by a rising sequence and involving a slight change of rhythm on the words 'For all honour and blessing and power' before the final climax comes with the slowing down of the tune's pace on the words 'Jesus Christ, Son of the Living God'.

E.g. 19 *Jesus shall take the highest honour*[57]

Richards's 'There is Power in the name of Jesus' is an entire tune waiting for a climax, and he doesn't let us down. The last three words cover six bars, and the melody which has been steadily rising from the beginning to an intermediate climax halfway through on the word 'saved' (four beats on a high E), rises again to the top keynote on the appropriate words 'There is no other name that is higher than Jesus'.

E.g. 20 *There is Power in the name of Jesus*[58]

57 SH98, no. 77.
58 SH98 no. 129.

Other Characteristics

It is also worth looking out for the way in which harmony or accompaniment can transform a very unremarkable tune. We have already seen how in some contemporary music, such as that from the Vineyard, or the compositions of Smith, the competence of the band and their improvisation can be what keeps a bland melodic line going. However, it is equally true of some traditional tunes, particularly from the Victorian era, that it is the harmony which has helped them survive. Most notable is the popular tune actually called *Deep Harmony* ('Sweet is the work').[59] Here, the first line of melody concludes with four identical notes, in fact the first half of the tune only contains five notes. *St. Chrysostom* ('Jesus, my Lord, my God, my all') and *Rivaulx* ('Father of heaven, whose love profound'), are similar.[60]

Some of the contemporary songs, however, do display a strength and vigour which is derived from good harmonic progression. Take the two Bowater tunes discussed above, for example. 'Jesus shall take the highest honour', is an unremarkable enough melody, but an ascending bass and a flattened seventh in the accompaniment between the first and second lines keep the tune flowing well. A series of diminished and augmented chords accompanying a simple four note melodic motif performs the same function in 'Lamb of God'. One piece in SH98, 'Calm me Lord',[61] seems almost unsingable at first glance, but is worth knowing. The harmonic sequences are a good atmospheric background to the theme of the words in what is essentially a short devotional piece. It is bravely atonal.

Every genre has its musical trademarks and I have noticed an increasing dependence on major 7th chords, particularly in the mellow pieces.[62] These can be effective, but can become tiresome and predictable if this is the only style used in worship.

---

[59] *Mission Praise*, no. 620.
[60] *Hymns for Today's Church*, nos. 476, 359.
[61] SH98, no. 16.
[62] This is particularly true of Bowater's music. See SH98, nos. 22, 83.

One way in which the contemporary worship song has been greatly influenced by the form of the traditional gospel song is in the trait of having a 'catchy' chorus preceded by a less memorable or bland verse. Older songs such as 'Living he loved me', 'He lives', and 'Because he lives', all exist in some hymnals as choruses in their own right, even though they pre-existed with verses attached. Kendrick's 'Shine, Jesus, Shine', and 'We shall stand',[63] are both recognised by their strong rhythmic choruses and although, particularly in the case of the former, the music of the verses may have more to commend them technically, there is little doubt that it is the strength of the refrains that have made them both so popular.[64]

Now it is time to turn from technical analysis to some general observations on the state of the church's current canon of praise, and to look at three specific developments in recent worship music: namely, the Spring Harvest publications, the output from the Iona community and, more briefly, some of the hymns of Christopher Idle.

---

[63] *Mission Praise*, nos. 445, 737.
[64] See J. M. Frame, *Contemporary Worship Music*, pp. 118–121, for a more detailed musical analysis of 'Shine, Jesus, Shine'.

Chapter 5

Are We the People?
Triumph and Victory in the Songs of Spring Harvest

I'll be frank from the outset. The standard of contemporary worship songs is embarrassingly low. In spite of much talk about the great new wave of songwriters that has emerged, when one takes time to examine the theological depth and literary quality of the songs in question, one is left with an over-riding sense of shallowness, sentimentality and sameness. The songs may be popular, even catchy, and the writers may have earned their reputations as competent guitar players (usually) and leaders of worship at mainstream evangelical events; however, it seems that in many cases their reputation far exceeds the worthiness of their compositions.

Let me reiterate: I am not a traditionalist. I believe strongly that new songs should be written, and written in abundance to engage with the musical language of the modern era, and that they should be played on whatever combination of instruments is appropriate, loud or soft, raucous or mellow. My criticism stems not from some principled objection to contemporary genres or styles; it is born out of frustration. Frustration that people who have undoubted musical talent can be content to write lyrics which are so undemanding and mediocre. Let me justify these rather harsh comments.

A survey of some recent Spring Harvest Worship Books[1] (SH) will serve to illustrate my points. The SH Worship book, updated annually, is the main source of worship material for thousands of fellowship groups, new churches and worship

---

[1]   The songs evaluated here all come from the 1996-8 books: *Spring Harvest Praise 1996/7/8*, Uckfield: Spring Harvest, 1996-8.

teams within mainline churches. In fact, for thousands of individuals it serves as their only current 'hymn-book'.[2] This means that the weaknesses of this book will not be balanced by the strengths of another. Let me highlight the following major problems with having such a restricted diet.

a) Total domination of one era and style

Of the 160 songs in SH97, for instance, 63 (40%) were written in the last two years, 101 (63%) were written in the last five years, while only 19 (12%) were 'traditional hymns' written before 1980. The proportions for 1998 are virtually the same: of 163 songs, 61 (37%) were written in the last two years, 106 (65%) in the last five years, with only 20 (12%) written before 1980. In recent years there has been a bit of a resurgence in the inclusion of older hymns in these compilations, although I notice that the number in SH96 (26 [16%]) was a little higher. While I acknowledge that the Spring Harvest festival exists partly as a stage for new songs, there needs to be a recognition that it has become more than a two week retreat, and has, intentionally or not, become one of the biggest influences on the current canon of praise. Recently some other events, also from within the charismatic milieu, such as Stoneleigh and Soul Survivor—a specifically youth-orientated event, where Matt Redman emerged as a worship leader—may claim to have comparable influence musically. However, the Spring Harvest collection contains the most popular pieces from these other events, and largely due to the publication and wide distribution of the annual worship book still remains the main means by which these songs get accepted in the mainstream.

This being so, the recovery and inclusion of more hymns from the church of previous generations must be a priority. Those that are currently included tend to be a little predictable: 'Amazing grace',[3] 'And Can it Be?', 'Crown him

---

2   In North America the parallel publication would be the *Maranatha Music Praise Chorus Book* (Word publishing), which is the publication Frame uses for his critiques.

3   SH97, no. 6.

with many crowns', 'When I survey'.[4] They are arranged with modern introductions and unison lines in a manner which would make a purist blush, but that is a small price to pay, and probably a necessary one, in order to save them from extinction. The main problem with the domination of the new is that the collection lacks variety and depth. By the time one reads up to number 150, it is almost possible to compose the next song oneself. John Frame makes a similar point regarding the endless series of tapes and CDs emanating from Christian Music publishing houses.[5]

b) Homocentricity

There is a prevailing homocentricity about the material. This is not a generalisation. 59 (42%) of the post-1980 songs in SH97 had what I would call an *overt* concentration on the first person: how *we* are worshipping, what *our* needs are and how Jesus satisfies *my* longings. Again, there is nothing wrong with this *per se*, but 42% is too high when one bears in mind that many of the others also had a strong, but not dominant, personal dimension. In 1998 the number had dropped to around 50 (35%), but this is still high, and I noticed a particular, rather unbalanced, emphasis on what God does *for me*, seen in the recurrence of the word 'need'. These are just a few examples:

> I need you like dew in the desert, like refreshing summer rain,
> Come and pour your love again on me.
> I'm finding that every time I come and ask for something more
> You never fail to pour your love on me.[6]

> I need you more, more than yesterday;
> I need you more, more than words can say,
> I need you more than ever before, I need you Lord.[7]

---

4   SH98, nos. 5, 21, 150.
5   J. Frame, *Contemporary Worship Music*, p. 40.
6   SH98, no. 59.
7   SH98, no. 60.

My Jesus, my lifeline,
I need you more than I've ever known.[8]

Surround me, defend me,
O how I need you.
To you I lift up my soul.[9]

Say the word, I will be healed;
You are the great physician,
you meet every need.[10]

Let me emphasise that I do not believe there is anything wrong with declaring our need for Christ—indeed there is something amiss with us if we don't. Similarly, some of the Psalms demonstrate the importance of the personal, experiential, and even introspective dimension in worship. My point here is that there is a lack of balance and a definite man-centred orientation about the collection as a whole. This may not at first be obvious since so much worship music does emphasise the exaltation and glory of Christ (see below), and the vast majority of the songs are directed towards God. However, rather than reflecting on the nature of God, these songs that I have described as 'homocentric' concentrate on our experience of God. This is fine in itself, but acknowledging this orientation should lead us to look elsewhere for songs of greater breadth and wider themes.

Even songs which purport to be about God often lapse into introspection. For example, 'The Power of your Love' is an excellent song and a powerful tune with a good use of musical climax both at the end of the verse and chorus ('the power of your love'), and at the beginning of the chorus where the hitherto flowing tune is appropriately 'held back' on the words 'Hold me now'. However, the weakness comes towards the end where a rather over-used biblical image in modern worship (that makes no real connection with anything which has gone before) makes way for the strange notion of the worshipper soaring *with* God.

---

8   SH98, no. 99.
9   SH98, no. 137.
10   SH98, no. 118.

Lord, I come to you, let my heart be changed
....and as I wait, I'll rise up like the eagle,
And I will soar with you....[11]

c) Too many songs by too few writers

This has always been a danger of hymnbooks through the ages. But in SH97 there are 52 songs (33%) by only four writers or writing teams: Graham Kendrick, the Richards duo, Matt Redman and Martin Smith. In SH98 this percentage has been reduced to 25%, although if the contributions of Chris Bowater and Dave Bilborough are included the figure rises to 31% from just six writers. The frustrating thing is that only rarely are the contributions of these writers among the best in the volumes. Kendrick, of course, is a widely respected writer some of whose output will last for decades, but it is quite clear from looking at the new offerings in SH96-8 that very little here matches the depth of 'Meekness and Majesty' or 'The Servant King.'[12] Instead he seems to have become tied into a rather tiresome 'call and response' technique which can reduce the worshippers to chanting only one or two lines for an entire song:

Leader	The younger to the older say,	*All*	'Oh the Lord is good'.
	We want to hear you say,		'The Lord is good'.
	Older to the younger say,		'Oh the Lord is good'.
	We want to hear you say,		'The Lord is good'.[13]

And that was verse 4! In contrast to the wealth of scriptural imagery in for example 'Rejoice' or 'Make Way', his later offerings are noticeably weak.

Jesus' love has got under our skin (x4)
Deeper than colour, oh richer than culture,

---

[11]   SH98, no. 87. Let me emphasise that I think this is generally a good and powerful song, and I include it in the appendix. However, my view that the use of the eagle image is unnecessary and possibly distracting has been enhanced by the fact that some younger members of my congregation insist on referring to this piece as 'The Birdie Song'!

[12]   *Mission Praise*, nos. 465, 162.

[13]   SH97, no. 103. See also 'Celebrate', no. 19.

> Oh stronger than emotion, oh wider than the ocean.
> Oh don't you want to celebrate, and congratulate somebody?
> Talk about a family! It's under our skin, under our skin.

Leader Everybody say love,   *All* Love!
Leader Everybody say love,   *All* Love! *etc.*[14]

Only in the very lyrical 'No scenes of stately majesty' does he come close to the gripping imagery of 'Come and See' (see below), or the plaintive meditation of 'Who can sound?'[15] Here are the first two verses, the other three are equally strong.

> No scenes of stately majesty, for the King of kings;
> No nights aglow with candle-flame, for the King of love;
> No flags of empire hung in shame, for Calvary;
> No flowers perfumed the lonely way
> That led him to a borrowed tomb for Easter Day.
>
> No wreaths upon the ground were laid, for the King of kings;
> Only a crown of thorns remained, where he gave his love;
> A message scrawled in irony—'King of the Jews',
> Lay trampled where they turned away
> And no-one knew that it was the first Easter Day.[16]

Matt Redman and Martin Smith are undoubtedly two of 'the new Kendricks' in terms of profile. But although Redman's 'I will offer up my life' and 'Once again'[17] are undeniably superb songs, his other contributions, along with virtually all of Smith's, are sadly among the most worrying and problematic in the book (see sections f) and g) below). Preachers have long been aware of the subtle temptations that come with being 'on stage' and 'high profile'. In a culture where music has now usurped the spoken word as the dominant form of influence, those who lead worship face similar dangers, not least in the uncritical way that much of what they write gains a wide hearing, simply because of their reputation rather than the quality of the song.

---

14   SH97, no. 79.
15   *Mission Praise*, no. 766.
16   SH98, no. 102.
17   SH97, nos. 65, 74.

These men are the preachers to a generation, and that is why it is so vital to examine closely exactly what is being preached. In so doing it may at times be difficult not to appear over-critical of individuals who are undoubtedly fine Christians and gifted musicians. In some respects the fault lies not with writers such as Redman, whose material is probably the most hyped, but with the popular Christian press and the demands of what has become a lucrative industry. One Christian periodical recently wrote: 'Twenty-four year old Matt Redman has emerged in the last four years to be a modern day Charles Wesley'. It then quoted another musician as saying that 'his song "The Heart of Worship" [is] the most important song to be written in the last decade'.[18] Bold claims, although a comparative reading of 'Undignified' and 'And Can it Be'[19] should be sufficient to show the preposterous nature of such propaganda.

d) Theologically lightweight

Out of the 140 contemporary songs in SH97, apart from two which were loosely creedal, only six mentioned the resurrection, five dealt with creation, four with the second coming, three with the incarnation, two with forgiveness, while the faithfulness of God, the uniqueness of Jesus, and the high priesthood of Christ merited a solitary mention. I could only find one song which referred to the judgment of God. The atonement fared slightly better (around 14 songs) but often this was limited to a simple reference to the cross. By far the most prevalent theme is that of glorification and exaltation. At least 23 songs refer to the exalted Christ, while almost 20 deal with the power of God. In the 1998 collection the quantities are virtually the same, although Andy Piercy and Dave Clifton's 'This is the Sweetest Mystery'[20] is a fine reflection on the Trinity, and an example of how, with a bit of thought, contemporary worship songwriters can deal with

---

18 *The Little Acorn*, Issue 19, p. 33.
19 SH98, nos. 63, 5.
20 SH98, no. 133

profound theological themes within the necessary restrictions of the genre.

> This is the sweetest mystery,
> That you, O Lord are one in three;
> Majestic, glorious Trinity of Father, Spirit, Son;
> The heavenly Father, Great I AM,
> The Son of God, the Son of Man,
> And yet within this wondrous plan:
> The Spirit with us here.

Having outlined the wonders of the doctrine, the composers move to apply it in the second verse:

> Lord, may this truth become a flame
> That burns within our hearts....

There are, surprisingly, only a few songs dealing with the Second Coming, and here there is often confusion about whether the songwriter is speaking of the final return of Christ, or a coming revival. Take Robin Mark's popular 'Days of Elijah', for instance:

> These are the days of Elijah,
> Declaring the Word of the Lord;
> And these are the days of your servant, Moses,
> Righteousness being restored.
> And though these are days of great trial,
> Of famine and darkness and sword,
> Still we are the voice in the desert crying
> 'Prepare ye the way of the Lord'
>> Behold he comes riding on the clouds,
>> Shining like the sun, at the trumpet call....[21]

Similarly in Matt Redman's 'Believer', a line expressing his hope to witness the *parousia* is followed by lines appropriate only to an earthly revival:

> I hope to see you come down,
> Rend the mighty heavens,
> And let your glory cover all the earth;

---

[21] SH98, no. 131.

To see your sons and daughters
Come to know and love you,
And find a purer passion in the church.[22]

A look at the Topical Index of both SH97 and SH98 will further illustrate the general imbalance of themes. There are two columns on 'Praise and Thanksgiving', a column on 'Heart Worship', over 20 songs on 'Spiritual Warfare' and even a section devoted to 'March for Jesus'! In contrast 'Suffering and Trials' merits only 13 songs (16 in SH98) and 'The Church' only 7 (10 in SH98). Major themes such as the Incarnation, Resurrection and Second Coming don't feature as topics.

The movement away from a more balanced Christology and towards an emphasis on the exaltation of Christ can be seen in the development of Kendrick's writing. Several years ago, he was known for lyrics such as these:

Meekness and majesty, manhood and deity
In perfect harmony, the man who is God.

He walked where I walk, he stood where I stand,
He felt what I feel, he understands.[23]

Now his songs tend to focus much more on glorification, while at the same time being essentially homocentric.

So let us sing together in harmony,
And make the joyful sound of unity;
And as we worship Jesus we want the world to see his glory,
Reach out and take a hand and welcome one another.[24]

This trend raises some important questions. Are we in danger of concentrating on the 'otherness' of Jesus at the expense of his identification with us in the incarnation? Do we want the power of God, but not a share in the weakness and suffering of Christ? Can these 'glory songs' give the impression that we are worshipping a distant deity, rather than One who has become

---

22 SH98, no. 56.
23 *Mission Praise*, nos. 465, 221.
24 SH97, no. 113.

flesh? How exclusively Christian are some of the songs which speak only of adoring the 'high and exalted one', especially if they are sparse on the reasons for such adoration?

If we contrast some of these songs with older hymns on the same theme, their inadequacies are even more obvious. 'Rejoice the Lord is King', 'At the Name of Jesus', 'The head that once was crowned with thorns', and 'Look, you saints, the sight is glorious'[25] all leave us in no doubt as to why this Jesus is worthy of our praise. Furthermore, we are often led to the glorified Christ having had a glimpse of the suffering Servant.

One researcher has discovered that there has been a noticeable change in hymn themes in the last half-century. He surveyed one popular book looking particularly for songs dealing with the subject of problems and trials in the Christian life. By selecting over 130 words or images that hymnwriters have used to describe the form, effects or response to troubles, he discovered that while around 40% of the pre-1950 songs *that have survived and are in use today*, deal in some way with this general theme, only about 10% of post-1950 songs do so. He then shows that this is not indicative of an unhealthy melancholic orientation among older hymnwriters. Rather, the rich diversity of images and terms used, coupled with the fact that the vast majority of the hymns progress beyond the suffering to speak of reliance on God and hope of heaven, show that these writers acknowledged the reality of pain and struggle while believing that it was still possible, indeed necessary, to praise and trust God in the midst of it. It should also be noted that this survey did not take into account any pieces written after 1983. An updated survey would, I imagine, come up with similar conclusions.[26]

None of my comments are an attempt to idealise the past. John Frame makes the valid point that many traditional hymns can cover too much doctrine too quickly and that slower meditative worship songs concentrating on perhaps only one theme can actually teach the truth more

---

[25] *Mission Praise*, nos. 575, 41, 647, 426.

[26] I am grateful to Dr Tim Prescott for his reflections on this, and for letting me see his unpublished paper 'An Unhelpful Tendency in Modern Spiritual Songs', Dublin, 1998.

successfully.[27] Older hymns need linguistic revision, and perhaps even severe musical reconstruction if they are to be meaningful. However, what I'm trying to illustrate here, is the comparative paucity of theological content in the contemporary canon of praise. It has to be said that an exception to this in SH97 is Kendrick's excellent and moving 'Come and See',[28] but it is interesting to note that this was written in 1989. It is also encouraging to notice a couple of hymns by Christopher Idle in SH98, but more of him later.

e) An intimacy bordering on the erotic

The Song of Solomon has exercised the minds of exegetes, Jewish and Christian, for thousands of years. Whether we wish to take an overtly typological approach to the book or not, we cannot get away from the fact that the book's presence in the canon shows us that there is an appropriate place for an intimate expression of love in our relationship with God. Several of the songs in SH98 display what I would call an intimacy bordering on eroticism. Again this is a question of balance. I do not want to go as far as to say that none of these songs should ever be used. But I am concerned that, bearing in mind the theological deficiencies of this collection of worship music as a whole which I highlight in section g) below, and bearing in mind too the sexually explicit culture in which we live, these images and expressions may be misunderstood, and not everyone will feel comfortable using them in a corporate worship context. Sometimes the lyrics echo strongly the words of the biblical book:

> My first love is a blazing fire,
> I feel his powerful love in me;
> For he has kindled a flame of passion,
> And I will let it grow in me.
> And in the night I will sing your praise, my love.
> And in the morning I'll seek your face, my love.[29]

---

[27] *Contemporary Worship Music*, pp. 102–4.
[28] SH97, no. 20.
[29] SH98, no. 96.

On other occasions they seem to be echoing ordinary secular love-songs:

> Face to face, heart to heart,
> Letting your love touch every part....
> Face to face, hand in hand,
> Hearing you say 'I understand'.
> Here with you, my love, my friend,
> Savouring the time, not wanting it to end.[30]

> Father, I love the way
> You hold me close and say my name.[31]

> What a friend I've found
> Closer than a brother;
> I have felt your touch,
> More intimate than lovers.[32]

> You are my passion, love of my life,
> Friend and companion, my lover.
> All of my being longs for your touch,
> With all my heart I love you.[33]

And on yet other occasions the potency of the imagery is shocking and inappropriate:

> Kiss me with your healing touch,
> Take me to the heat of your fire,
> Bathe me in your liquid love,
> Oh saturate me, saturate me.[34]

f) Triumphalism

A noticeable and worrying development in many of the songs is that of triumphalism. This can take the form of a glorifying of this generation, a hyped-up expectation of a particular type of revival, or the anticipation that God is going to do something new and historically significant through today's

---

30 SH98, no. 22.
31 SH98, no. 27.
32 SH98, no. 149.
33 SH98, no. 159.
34 SH98, no. 64.

church. This is what Frame calls 'temporal chauvenism', the belief that our era is superior to all previous ones.[35] At least 35 of the contemporary songs in SH97 (25%) had this tendency. It is common in Richards and Redman and characteristic of virtually all of Smith's songs.

> Are we the people who will see God's kingdom come?
> ...Keep moving on, last generation.[36]

> Can we walk upon the water, if our eyes are fixed on you?
> There's an air of faith within us for a time of breaking through.
> Can we fly a little higher, can we soar on eagle's wings?
> ...Can we fly a little higher? (x4) [37]

> Did you feel the mountains tremble, did you hear the oceans roar?
> When the people rose to sing of Jesus Christ, the risen One?
> ...And here we see that, God, you're moving,
> A time of jubilee is coming, when young and old return to Jesus.[38]

> Father of Creation, unfold your sovereign plan:
> Raise up a chosen generation that will march through the land,
> ...O God, let this be the hour.[39]

> I'm going to be a history-maker in this land,
> ...We'll see miracles, we'll see angels sing,
> We'll see broken hearts making history.[40]

> It's rising up from coast to coast,
> ...Can this be the new day of praise,
> ...We have heard the Lion's roar,
> That speaks of heaven's love and power;
> Is this the time, is this the call?
> That ushers in your kingdom's rule? [41]

> We want to change this world, (x4)
> So wave those flags of justice over the nations,

---

[35] *Contemporary Worship Music*, p. 46.
[36] SH98, no. 6.
[37] SH97, no. 18.
[38] SH97, no. 25.
[39] SH97, no. 32.
[40] SH98, no. 70.
[41] SH98, no. 71.

And hit those drums of peace among the peoples,
We hear the sound of history in the making.[42]

Step by step we're moving forward,
Little by little taking ground.[43]

Living on the edge of destiny,
Looking in the face of promises;
We've never been this way before,
It could even be today.
Breaking through the haze of apathy,
Dawns a new day of expectancy;
We've never been this way before,
It could even be today.
Today, let this be the day....[44]

We must work together,
Bringing in the kingdom,
Bringing heaven here on earth.
Start a new world order,
Start a revolution,
Let all people know their worth.
We'll see it all, we'll see it all, we'll see it all....[45]

Sometimes the ground on which the song's hope of revival is based is rather flimsy:

I feel it in my spirit, I feel it in my bones,
You're going to send revival, bring them all back home.[46]

And, bearing in mind the persecutions that visit the church daily in other parts of the world, one wonders how helpful it is for upper middle-class Westerners to sing, perhaps a little glibly, 'We've been through fire, we've been through rain; we've been refined by the power of his name'?[47] This could also be said of the Richards's 'Love songs from Heaven,'[48] with its

---

42 SH98, no. 145.
43 SH97, no. 141.
44 SH98, no. 85.
45 SH98, no. 141.
46 SH98, no. 8
47 From Martin Smith's 'Men of Faith' SH98, no. 94.
48 SH98, no. 92.

line 'For you we live and for you we may die', although the statement in verse 2 that 'Blood of the martyrs has made your church strong' is a welcome reminder of how all is not sweetness, light and triumph in the Christian life.

In addition there are lyrics like this which don't actually say anything worthwhile:

> Down the mountain the river flows,
> And it brings refreshing wherever it goes;
> Through the valleys and over the fields,
> The river is rushing and the river is here.
> The river of God sets our feet a-dancing....[49]

Smith's 'Revival Town', which due to the popularity of his band *Delirious* has become something of a late 90s Christian youth-culture anthem, is probably the best example of this triumphalism. One may be able to excuse it as a concert number, given the necessary hype attached to live gigs, but it has made its way into SH98 and is being sung in worship services nationwide:

> Well, I've got a message to bring,
> I can't preach but I can sing
> And me and my brothers here
> Gonna play redemption hymns.
> We're not on our own, you know,
> It's all around the world;
> 'Cause this is the freedom generation,
> Living for revival in this time....
> Revival Town, that's what they're calling this place now:
> Revival Town, it'll put a smile on your face now,
> Revival Town.[50]

The problem with such lyrics is that when the revival doesn't come, or dies away, and faith is hard to sustain, the singers will be left feeling that they've been sold a lie and, like Elijah under his broom tree, will cry out in depression that they are no better than their fathers' generation (1Kgs 19:4). This potential problem is exacerbated when lyrics of such unfounded

---

[49] SH97, no. 27.
[50] SH98, no. 147.

expectations are placed alongside lyrics of extreme devotion and uncompromising commitment: 'I won't stop loving you', 'Every step I take is a step of faith', 'Forever I'll love you, forever I'll stand', 'I will love you come what may', 'Wholehearted, wholehearted in my praise to you.'[51]

Now, these are admirable sentiments and they should, of course, be sung. However, if they are not balanced with a theology of sin and forgiveness and an understanding of how to live when love grows cold and mistakes are made, then the likelihood of disillusionment and heartbreak is greater. The combination of such intimate devotion and an exaggerated (almost arrogant) sense of the importance of our generation, paves the way for a most unhealthy spirituality, resembling more the seed that fell among thorns than that which bore fruit (Luke 8:14-15).

g) Bad theology, cliché and careless writing

Sometimes individual songs cross the line from triumphalistic exuberance to appalling self-indulgence, as in Redman's 'Undignified', or perfectionism, as in the second and third example:

> I will dance, I will sing, to be mad for my King.
> ...And I'll become even more undignified than this.
> Na na na na na hey (x7) Here I, here I, here I, here I go.[52]

> You do all things well, just look at our lives.[53]

> (We're) Standing in all purity. [54]

Overall, the contemporary corpus is heavily cliché-ridden with spiritual terms often inserted with no thought of overall message or context. For example, if there is a weakness in Redman's 'I will offer up my life', it is surely the confused phraseology of the opening two lines:

---

[51] SH97, nos. 37, 61, 94, 149, 155.
[52] SH98, no. 63.
[53] SH98, no. 39.
[54] SH97, no. 124.

I will offer up my life in spirit and truth,
Pouring out the oil of love as my worship to you.[55]

Whereas Scripture speaks of worshipping in Spirit and truth and uses the imagery of God anointing us with the oil of gladness or oil of joy, this lyric is a little bit of a 'mix-and-match', which sounds fine until one stops to analyse what it is really trying to say. In Andy Piercy's 'We Worship and adore You', he writes:

The tongues of men and angels we need
To sing your praise,
So that we may glorify your name
Through heaven's eternal days.[56]

Again, the first line contains a well-known biblical phrase from 1Corinthians 13:1, but to say that in order to praise God we need something which Paul says is immaterial without love is to miss completely the point of the original biblical context. In Martin Smith's 'Did you hear the mountains tremble?' a Scriptural allusion to Psalm 24 is most inappropriately finished as the music of his band appears to take the place of the King of Glory:

Fling wide you heavenly gates,
Open up the doors and let the music play.[57]

One can see the same 'cut-and-paste' tendency in what is otherwise an excellent piece by Irish songwriter Robin Mark:

I praise you for your faithfulness, O Lord,
And for your Father's love that never fails;
Who am I? The King of love my Shepherd is;
Who am I, that you should call me friend?[58]

---

[55] SH98, no. 66.
[56] SH98, no. 144.
[57] SH97, no. 25. And what exactly is the thinking behind the line 'When people pray / Cloudless skies will break'?
[58] Unpublished. See also the example quoted at the end of the section on structure in chapter 3. For a good example of how to use an existing

Here the insertion of the famous hymn-title is totally incongruous. For a start the original line is poetically archaic with the 'is' at the end, and secondly, the words are unrelated to anything before or after. Occasionally the thoughtless use of biblical terms leads to some confusing theology, as in 'Jesus, now justified, his kingdom comes.' [59]

I have referred earlier to the thoughtless use of rural and nature images in many of the songs, and in SH98 I noticed a particular propensity for the metaphor of rain.

> His tears have fallen like rain on my life,
> Each drop a fresh revelation.[60]

> Wash my sins away in this falling rain.
> In this day of grace fill me once again.[61]

Joel Pott's 'Love Rain Down' is not only an example of confused and mixed metaphors (the rain is seen variously as our prayers and God's love, and somehow the rain is going to be encouraged by the lighting of a fire), but also contains the rather strange (and frightening) notion of our hearts being used as fuel for the fire. Since this metaphor is not developed or explained and fire in Scripture more often refers to judgment than to revival, this song produces more questions than answers in the worshippers' minds (presuming the worshippers are thinking about what they are singing in the first place).

> Let it rain, let it rain, let it rain, let it rain on every nation (x2).
> Take our hearts as fuel for the fire,
> Now is the time to see your power,
> Take our prayers as abundant rain,
> Open up the floodgates of heaven,

---

hymn title, see 'Ride on, ride on' by Bell/Maule, *Enemy of Apathy*, Glasgow: Wild Goose Publications, 1990, p. 25.

[59] SH97, no. 75. On a more minor note, one also finds a sprinkling of bad grammar: 'When there's hard times'(no. 149) and bad poetic emphasis: 'More than life-giving food the hungry dream of' (no. 90).

[60] SH98, no. 118.

[61] SH98, no. 89.

Let the trumpet sound and the rain come down.
Love rain down, down on me....[62]

In summary, one may justifiably ask if an individual song should be expected to be doctrinally comprehensive. The answer is 'of course not'. But neither should it be incomplete, misleading, or spend a lot of time saying not very much. I have tried to view this corpus of material as a whole, and am commenting on the lack of clear definition *anywhere* in the collection, and the tendency to be content with lyrics that 'sound right', rather than with those that are illuminating and accurate. At best no harm is done, but opportunities have been missed. After surveying the material, I am left with the impression that with a little more effort, songwriters who are certainly not without talent musically could enhance their work substantially by employing a little more lyrical creativity and a less restricted theological vision.

It is worth making one further observation. Aside from the depth of his words, Kendrick's genius musically lay in the way he was able, in the late 70s and early 80s, to bring into the worship arena the musical style he had formerly hammered out on the anvil of the concert hall. His influences were clearly the contemporary musicians of that period. Now that he has been immersed in the Christian scene for so long, it seems his musical writing has suffered. Furthermore, it is this Christian worship scene as it has developed over the past decade or so, rather than any external contemporary musical style, which seems to be the major influence on the emerging writers such as Redman and Smith. This being so, while their popularity within the Christian circuit may remain high, we should not be surprised that their compositions will appear to be more self-consciously introspective, and that Christian worship music generally will seem to have lost an important cutting-edge.

Unfortunately I have had to concentrate on the negative aspects of the contemporary worship-song, simply because so much of it is being sung and being accepted uncritically. There are of course several very fine pieces among the Spring Harvest

---

[62]   SH98, no. 84.

corpus and even some of the ones I have referred to have their redeeming qualities. A look at the final chapter and Appendix will show that I see the Spring Harvest collection as a useful and valuable resource from which to select worship pieces, but a resource with inadequacies which have to be compensated for through the use of other material. The big danger is that we become lazy and uncritical. It is not just traditionalists that revert to their comfort zone rather than engaging in creative and thoughtful analysis. The unquestioning adoption of the next Spring Harvest book as the authoritative canon of praise, can be as debilitating to growth through worship as a rigorous adherence to the liturgical forms of Cranmer's Book of Common Prayer.

Chapter 6

Love From Below:
Incarnation and Atonement in Iona and Idle

THE IONA COMMUNITY

The Iona Community in Scotland have published several books over the last decade. They have not gained anything like as wide an acceptance as the broadly charismatic Spring Harvest songs, although some have found their way into denominational hymnbooks and supplements. Ten of Bell's pieces can be found in *Glory to God*,[1] the hymnal supplement of the Presbyterian Church in Ireland, and seventeen in *Common Ground*,[2] an ecumenical Scottish contemporary anthology. In that nearly all stem from the pens of John Bell and Graham Maule,[3] an unvaried diet of Iona material would of course be as unhealthy as an unvaried diet of anything else. However, there is not the same expectation that these books will become the hymnal of a fellowship or church in the same way as Spring Harvest fulfils that function. Instead, they are resources to supplement existing hymnals, and very good resources at that.

Although the body of songs as a whole could be open to the opposite criticism of a heavy concentration on the humanity of Christ, there are few of the lyrics which could not be used by churches of whatever theological persuasion. However valid or invalid accusations of pantheism and universalism may be regarding some groups who have

---

1   Oxford: OUP, 1994.
2   Edinburgh: St Andrew Press, 1998.
3   Apart from the collections of 'world songs' in, for example, *Many and Great*, Glasgow: Wild Goose Publications, 1990.

espoused or adopted aspects of Celtic spirituality, those accusations cannot be substantiated with regard to these excellent songs which, as I make clear, help us to recover the wonder of 'God made man'. There is possibly a weakness in the material as a whole in terms of a comprehensive theology of the atonement. The pieces are good at presenting the horror and wonder of the crucifixion, but the substitutionary nature of the atonement is not so much neglected as understated. This, however, is where the hymns of Idle discussed below can complement Bell. Space only permits a cursory glance at the riches available in the Iona material, but one is struck immediately by the powerful poetry, careful composition and the theological insight of many of the songs.

As already mentioned, few contemporary worship songs deal well with the subject of suffering and pain (just over 10 in SH97), and when it is mentioned, the suffering is often dismissed rather simplistically.

> On the battlefield, although the pain is real,
> My struggles soon will fade
> As his glory is revealed.[4]

Two songs which give a much better treatment of the subject would be 'Great is the Darkness', and 'Who can sound the depths of sorrow?'[5] The Bell/Maule songs, however, are permeated with images of struggle and pain, and an acknowledgement that 'life in the Spirit' does not mean an absence of such trouble.

> Today I affirm
> The Spirit within me,
> At worship and work,
> In struggle and rest.[6]

> Where minds and bodies reel with pain
> Which nervous smiles can never mask.

---

4   SH97, no. 96.
5   SH98, no. 34; *Mission Praise*, no. 766.
6   'Today I awake', *Love From Below*, Glasgow: Wild Goose Publications, 1992, p. 13.

...Where family life has lost its bliss
And silences endorse mistrust;
Or anger boils and tempers flare
As love comes under threat from lust.
...Ah God, you with the Maker's eye,
Can tell if all that's feared is real.
...Stretch out your hand to help your folk,
From stumbling blocks to stepping stones.[7]

God give us hope that lasts
Through passion, and through pain;
Through danger, doubt and death,
Till life is raised again.
When dread and pessimism loom
Direct us to the empty tomb.'[8]

Many contemporary worship songs dwell on the beauty of Jesus, often in a quite sentimental, if not sickening and unbiblical way; as one recent song puts it 'your beauty blows my mind'.[9] The clearly messianic Isaiah 53:2 speaks thus: 'He had no beauty or majesty to attract us to him, nothing in his appearance that we should desire him'. Yet some titles from the last couple of decades include: 'Isn't he beautiful', 'May the beauty of Jesus fill my life', 'O Lord, you're beautiful', 'You are beautiful beyond description'.[10] The last of these, which is, in all other respects, a fine song, is not as problematic in that it is eventually made clear that the adjectives refer to 'Holy God' rather than to Christ. Similarly, in Keith Green's 'O Lord, you're beautiful', another fine song, the referent is ambiguous although the second line 'your face is all I seek' recalls Psalm 27:4 and implies that the subject is indeed Yahweh. Nevertheless, in the other two cases the subject is clearly Christ and in all four the prominence given to the attribute of beauty could be misleading. While there is nothing wrong in affirming the internal beauty of perfect humanity as found in Christ, the titles mentioned above do not make clear that this is what they are referring to. Instead, through the unqualified

---

7   'Stumbling blocks and stepping stones', *Love From Below*, pp. 27-8.
8   'Gifts that last', *Love From Below*, p. 35.
9   From 'My Friend and King', SH98, no. 95.
10   *Mission Praise*, nos. 344, 788, 462, 513.

use of terms such as 'beautiful' they could appear, in our current cultural context, simply to be making a statement about the physical attributes of Christ, and painting a very different picture to that of Isaiah 53.

In powerful contrast, Bell/Maule's 'Emperor of fools' speaks of 'the monarch the world has wilted' and 'the gargoyle of grace, grotesquely hung in space'.[11] Their 'Carol of the Epiphany' meditates upon the humility of Christ's birth as seen through the eyes of the visiting Magi who (accepting the traditional view that there were three) each sing a verse:

> I sought him dressed in finest clothes,
> Where money talks and status grows;
> But power and wealth he never chose:
> It seemed he lived in poverty.[12]

Other songs develop the poverty theme with some marvellous images of the Bethlehem couple before and after the birth:

> Forced to make the tiresome journey
> Flanked by her redundant groom,
> All the brightness in her body
> Longs to end the godless gloom.[13]

> Not a well-established family
> With an heirloom christening shawl,
> But a homeless, wandering couple
> Parented the Lord of All.[14]

Similarly, in contrast to the triumphalism so in vogue elsewhere, and the increasing preoccupation within many contemporary Christian circles for headlines and 'bigness', these songs echo Christ's parable of the mustard seed (Luke 13:19), and remind us of the Gospel way:

---

11 *Enemy of Apathy*, Glasgow: Wild Goose Publications, 1990, p. 51.
12 *Innkeepers and Light Sleepers*, Glasgow: Wild Goose Publications, 1992, p. 50.
13 *Innkeepers and Light Sleepers*, p. 29.
14 *Innkeepers and Light Sleepers*, p. 40.

He knew the greatness of the small
Who spied two pennies in the plate...
He knew the beauty of the small
Who saw the sparrow in the sky...
He knew the weakness of the small
Who dandled babies on his knee...
And so the kingdom comes, he said,
In hidden ferment of the yeast,
In vagrants summoned to a feast....

When we defer to sight or size,
Believing big is always best;
And falling for the Tempter's test,
God open our eyes
To see how Christ, the Lord of all,
Smiles from the small.[15]

The songs are often well contextualised culturally, and I particularly liked the reference to the Bethlehem shepherds as 'crofters'.[16] Occasionally, however, the Scots terms are a little too obscure, for example 'handsel' in 'Look up and wonder',[17] and this may limit their value to a wider constituency.

When the songs do deal with the ascension and exaltation of Christ the contrast with the Spring Harvest songs is striking:

Forsaking chariots of fire
And fanfared brass,
As strangely silent as he came,
The Saviour leaves;
And God, with heaven's caress,
The Son receives.[18]

For Bell/Maule the subject of many of their songs is not Christ exalted in heaven, but Christ incarnate on earth. By concentrating on this (while not neglecting the other), they are filling an obvious gap in contemporary hymnody. These verses

---

[15] 'The greatness of the small', *Love from Below*, p. 63.
[16] *Innkeepers and Light Sleepers*, p. 45.
[17] *Innkeepers and Light Sleepers*, p. 32.
[18] *Enemy of Apathy*, p. 99.

from their 'Hymn of the Passion' demonstrate their poetic skill:

> Jesus, donkey-carried treasure, palm-waved prince, the people's pleasure
> Pounds to heaven in mangled measure: loud hosannas fill the sky.
>
> Jesus, temple-trade upsetter, gilt-edged greed needs every debtor;
> Rescue faith from human fetter: turn the tables, let love fly.
>
> Jesus, man of God, neglected; Jesus, God in man rejected,
> Crucified and unprotected: 'It is finished'! shout and die.[19]

Note also these lines on the obedience of Christ:

> Had you conformed, had you condoned, had you complied,
> None would be heard pricing your head, nursing their pride.[20]

There is a dramatic and atmospheric element to many of their songs, and our worship is enhanced as we understand more of the reality of what was involved, for example, in Palm Sunday or Good Friday:

> Ride on, ride on, the time is right,
> The roadside crowds scream with delight;
> Palm branches mark the pilgrim way,
> Where beggars squat and children play. [21]
>
> When the Son of God was dying, long ago.
> Some played dice and some knelt crying, lost and low.
> Cynics sneered and wagged their tongues,
> Mockers mimicked funeral songs....
>
> Humankind repeats Golgotha every day.
> God gets gagged while friend and followers
> Turn away. [22]

---

19 *Enemy of Apathy*, p. 33.
20 *The Courage to Say No*, Glasgow: Wild Goose Publications, 1996, p. 28.
21 *Enemy of Apathy*, p. 25.
22 *The Courage to Say No*, p. 35.

While images of the countryside dominate many of our older hymns (and mountains and rivers seem to occur regularly in modern songs too), there have been few hymns dealing with the urban life which most of the church worldwide experiences daily. Bell/Maule offer this:

> Praise the Lord with city voices
> Pitched in concrete, sweat and steel;
> Let the thousand urban choices
> Always bias to what's right and real....
> Praise the Lord as science advances
> Foundries roar, computers flair....[23]

Perhaps the most striking thing about the authors of the Iona songs is their courage to use earthy words, phrases or images which traditionally would be thought inappropriate for worship. Yet when one encounters these lyrics for the first time, they have such an emotional power that the superficiality of much of our other material is exposed:

> As if you were not there,
> We televise the dying,
> Watch the helpless victims crying....[24]

> In warm embrace for withered arms,
> In dining out with tarnished guests,
> In breaking umpteen petty rules,
> In controversial, quiet requests.
> Barriers dividing heaven from earth
> Were bulldozed to reveal our worth.[25]

And what pastor has not wished that there were hymns to help these people?—

> Feel for the parents who've lost their child,
> Feel for the women whom men have defiled. [26]

---

[23]   *Love from Below*, p. 99.
[24]   *Love from Below*, p. 73.
[25]   *Enemy of Apathy*, p. 67.
[26]   *Love from Below*, p. 67.

If we fear that this is too blatant, that such words overstep the marks of decency and propriety, then how do we deal with the offence of 'God with us'?

> We fear you God; You dare to come
> Offending from the virgin womb.
> Through this, and through the suckling breast,
> Our sense of decency you test,
> Till worldly life is weaned and blessed. [27]

The big disadvantage of much of this material is that many of the tunes are a little inaccessible for the average congregation. Certainly young people will not find them as immediately attractive as the Spring Harvest corpus. The latter are successful because they can be picked up easily by a guitarist, led confidently by a band, and are available on top-selling CDs in a Christian record store near you! Congregational participation is almost irrelevant. With the Iona songs, many are not conducive to guitar and some are encouraged to be sung unaccompanied and therefore they require a degree of confidence and hard work which is no bad thing, but which can mitigate against the ready acceptance of the pieces by a congregation or fellowship. The Iona books do offer alternative suggestions of well-known tunes to accompany the hymns. 'Ride On',[28] for example, will go to *Crasselius*, the traditional tune for 'Ride on, ride on in majesty', but this should not prevent Bell's vibrant, rhythmic and atmospheric tune from being used if the resources are there. As mentioned earlier, music should play a subordinate role in hymnody, but it is still an essential role, and it would be unfortunate if the riches of some Iona hymns were lost because either worship leaders lacked the will to teach them, or worshippers lacked the necessary musical expertise to sing them.

---

27 *Enemy of Apathy*, p. 59.
28 *Enemy of Apathy*, p. 25.

JUBILATE HYMNS AND CHRISTOPHER IDLE

The contemporary contributions found in *Hymns for Today's Church*, and similar publications stand somewhere between the two styles surveyed above. The writers tend to be of a different generation to Smith and Redman, write in the established metrical style, and deal with more traditional doctrinal topics in their hymns. One could not accuse their collections of being theologically unbalanced or lightweight. However, like the Iona material, they are unlikely to influence the emerging church as widely or rapidly as the Spring Harvest corpus. Nevertheless, their importance should not be overlooked. Hymns such as 'Tell out my Soul' and 'Lord for the Years' by Timothy Dudley-Smith, 'To him we come' by James Seddon and 'Christ Triumphant' by Michael Saward,[29] are already classics and will be in use for many years to come. In this respect they belong to the enduring rather than transient category of worship music discussed in chapter 8. Many of the pieces are fine poetically and theologically, although we should remember Frame's point about some hymns covering too much material too quickly.[30] Many of them do, however, deal in depth with the atonement and it may be of help to look briefly at the work of one of the writers, Christopher Idle, on this topic since this is where some have felt the Iona material to be weak.

Idle contributed 35 pieces to *Hymns for Today's Church,* and two of these deal specifically with the passion and death of Christ. There are few hymns about the trial of Christ, but Idle portrays it well and brings in the theological application in the final verse.[31]

---

[29] *Mission Praise*, nos. 631, 428, 709, 77. The tunes for two of these were written by Michael Baughan, and his contribution, along with John Barnard, David Peacock and Norman Warren should not be forgotten. Between them they provide almost 100 tunes for *Hymns for Today's Church*.

[30] See ch. 5 n. 27 above.

[31] *Hymns for Today's Church*, no. 129.

Verse 1:   He stood before the court
            On trial instead of us;
            He met its power to hurt,
            Condemned to face the cross:
            Our king, accused of treachery;
            Our God, abused for blasphemy.

The contrasts in the final two lines here remind us of the appalling illogicality and injustice of the trial. Poetically, Idle is choosing to employ a middle rhyme in the last two lines of each stanza, which is more demanding, but which he carries well through the whole hymn.

Verse 2:   These are the crimes that tell
            The tale of human guilt;
            Our sins, our death, our hell—
            On these the case is built:
            To this world's powers their Lord stays dumb;
            The guilt is ours, no answers come.

Verse 2 heightens the tension as the case is built up and we are made to feel personally our part in the drama.

Verse 3:   The sentence must be passed,
            The unknown prisoner killed;
            The price is paid at last,
            The law of God fulfilled:
            He takes our blame, and from that day
            The accuser's claim is wiped away.

Idle's use of short clauses, each beginning with 'the', suits the context of legal judgment, and the passing of the sentence. There is good alliteration in 'passed, prisoner, price, paid'.

Verse 4:   Shall we be judged and tried?
            In Christ our trial is done;
            We live, for he has died,
            Our condemnation gone:
            In Christ are we both dead and raised,
            Alive and free—his name be praised!

Although the earlier verses have been more than description (there is substitution in verse 1, sin in verse 2, satisfaction and atonement in verse 3) it is in this final verse that the application is driven home. We are justified and liberated and live in hope of resurrection; so the hymn ends with an appropriate exhortation to praise.

In 'Downtrodden Christ'[32] Idle structures the hymn around the hours of the first Good Friday: the crucifixion in verse 1, the eclipse in verse 2, and the death of Christ in verse 3. There is nothing particularly new in the treatment of theological theme, but the angle from which he approaches it is novel and refreshing, both in terms of the passage of time and the different postures of Christ: downtrodden, uplifted, outstretching.

> Downtrodden Christ, to you we pray
> Who at the third hour of the day
> Were led away and nailed up high
> In naked shame beneath the sky:
> > Show through the pain that scars your face
> > The love of God, and man's disgrace.
>
> Uplifted Christ, to you we pray
> Who at the sixth hour of the day
> Took all our guilt upon that tree
> In darkness, blood and agony:
> > Look on our pride and unbelief
> > Grant us repentance and relief.
>
> Outstretching Christ, to you we pray
> Who at the ninth hour of the day
> Alone dismissed your final breath
> And opened heaven by your death:
> > Come to our dying world and reign,
> > That we with you may live again.

In contrast to the short clauses that peppered his hymn on Christ's trial, here the sentences are long and the punctuation sparse, communicating the slowness of the death. Warren's lyrical tune also adds to the sense of suspended animation.

It was with particular pleasure that I noticed that a later hymn of Idle's and, to my mind, his best to date, has been

---

[32] *Hymns for Today's Church*, no. 125.

included in *Spring Harvest 98*. It also deals with the passion, and Kelly's tune is triumphant and stirring. The theme is not, this time, reflective wonder or penitential grieving, but assured victory. From the opening clause one is hit with the irony of singing about death in such an exuberant manner:

> Yes, finished! The Messiah dies,
> Cut off for sins, but not his own;
> Completed is the sacrifice,
> The great redeeming work is done.

The verse continues to expound the doctrine of justification and the second verse deals with reconciliation and the tearing down of barriers symbolised in the rending of the temple veil. His final two verses deal with the defeat of Satan, Christ's imputed righteousness and access to heaven in a manner which is sheer Wesley, although the creative final image from the world of property is a master-stroke:

> The reign of sin and death is done,
> And all may live, from sin set free;
> Satan and his pretended throne
> Are swallowed up in victory.
> Saved from the curse of God I am;
> My Saviour hangs upon a tree!
> See there the meek and silent Lamb;
> His final breath he breathes for me.
>
> In Christ accepted and brought near
> And clothed in righteousness divine,
> I see the path to life made clear,
> And all your merits, Lord, are mine.
> Death, hell and sin are now subdued,
> All grace is now to sinners given,
> And so I plead the atoning blood
> And claim the title deeds of heaven.[33]

It is gratifying that a piece of such robust theology is present in the latest contemporary worship-books and set to music that is like the more metrical of Kendrick and Richards rather than

---

[33] SH98, no. 157.

the traditional hymn-tune. I only hope that it is given the 'air-play' it deserves.[34]

THE CURRENT SCENE: A SUMMARY

It is difficult to know what the late twentieth century will be remembered for in terms of its contribution to congregational church music. Kendrick is good, but is still at his best when writing in the traditional hymn genre. Idle etc. are excellent but, like Bell, will not be immediately accessible (or even attractive) to many in the younger, emerging church. Spring Harvest have targetted this group, but we have outlined the significant weaknesses involved in using that material exclusively. The Vineyard have broken some new ground, but in so doing have pushed back the limits of what can be termed 'congregational song', and their limiting themselves to entirely home-grown material results in some expected ecclesiological and theological deficiencies.

It is important that we recognise that, at this moment in history, we have at our disposal a mine of good material. The compositions of previous centuries have been refined by time and we are left with gold which we discount to the detriment of ourselves and our churches. The compositions of the present, while yet unrefined, also contain gold among the dross. In our final section, we turn to the vital topic of how the wealth of material available to the contemporary church can best be pooled and utilised. How do we combine music, poetry and doctrinal truth so that believers are edified and encouraged to encounter the Living God? When it comes to selecting material for worship, what are the main issues which face those who are leading worship today?

---

[34] I'm disappointed to notice that it has been omitted from SH99.

Chapter 7

Worship Teams and One-Man Bands

I stated at the beginning that I believed that the battle to save the hymn had been lost. Looking at Britain and Ireland as a whole, and taking into account the many attending so-called 'new churches', it seems that increasing numbers of Evangelicals are unfamiliar with anything other than a few 'old favourites'. In line with parallel developments in other areas of contemporary culture, change is happening fast, and whatever battles may be raging within 'mainline' Kirk Sessions and committees, outside, and in other branches of the church, people are embracing the new (often uncritically) and many young Christians are unwilling to connect, or perhaps even culturally *incapable* of connecting with the world of the traditional hymn. Furthermore, technological changes have meant that hymnbooks are not necessarily required and therefore a vital connecting thread with the hymnody of the past is in danger of being severed. Hymnology, as traditionally understood, is a dying discipline. These are the facts. How do we meet the challenge they present? Let us look at these challenges by examining the personnel (the who?), the resources (the what?), and the methods (the how?) involved in conducting and leading praise today.

MINISTER OR MONOPOLISER?

The one abiding hope that the battle to blend the old and the new need not be lost for ever, resides in the leadership of the churches. God, in his wisdom, has entrusted the direction of his church to Spirit-filled men and women. Therefore these leaders or 'under-shepherds' have a responsibility to guide the flock not only in Christian lifestyle, prayer, vocation, ministry and mission, but also in praise and public worship. Nevertheless, guiding does not mean doing it all. Within the Presbyterian tradition, in keeping with most confessional branches of the church, responsibility for conducting public worship, including leading the praise, rests with the 'minister' or teaching elder.[1] However, this is a responsibility which can be, indeed should be, delegated, particularly if the minister has little or no musical expertise or knowledge of the wide variety of material available. A supervisory and encouraging role can still be maintained, but it is surely bad for both minister and congregation for the former to monopolise the leading of worship when more gifted and equally spiritual people are available within the body. Many ministers have stated their preference for leading the worship so they can 'get the feel' of the service before preaching. This is not a good enough reason potentially to stifle the gifts of others. The service does not exist solely for the minister's benefit but so that the congregation as a whole can meet with God. Perhaps if more ministers took a back seat and benefited from the skills of others in this area, their preaching would be significantly enhanced.

Let me emphasise that I am not encouraging the minister to abdicate all responsibilities in the area of worship. I am actually suggesting a more demanding and time-intensive role for the minister, involving the selection, equipping and mentoring of suitable people to assist in the leading of worship. Too many churches who have departed from the 'one-person show', have erred in the opposite direction by handing over full responsibility for worship to a group or team who may be adequate musicians but who neither know well the people whom they are meant to be leading in worship, nor have sufficient theological knowledge or Christian experience to raise the level of worship above a series of banal introductions and generalised prayers. Of course God can use and bless the ministry of a nervous, stuttering young Christian who gives

---

[1]   Hereafter referred to as 'the minister' purely for the sake of convenience.

words of testimony in between choosing a few favourite songs—and such occasions do the congregation good, because of the integrity and sincerity of the whole situation—but this should not be the limit of our ambition when it comes to worship; it should not be our staple diet.

One can sympathise with ministers who wish to lead worship all the time, on the grounds that it is they who know the people's needs, and who have spent time pastoring the flock from week to week. They want to engage in what is also a vital part of pastoral work, that of leading the people sensitively and meaningfully in worship. One also sympathises with church members who express a preference for this approach based on their respect for the minister, as opposed to the high 'cringe-factor' sometimes present when someone untrained and unpolished is leading. Such people have sometimes expressed to me an impatience and frustration with the cliché-ridden superficial comments of jovial worship leaders who exhort the congregation to 'just praise the Lord', or 'claim his victory', while they are nursing some real and deep hurts. If many have left mainline churches over the years because of a lack of life and joy in worship, there has been some traffic the other way because of the sterility and predictability of so-called open worship times where one can foretell the points in the service where these exhortations will be made (and the guitar chords which will be strummed to accompany them). However, I think these concerns can be met within a general equipping context and without reverting to ministerial monopolisation, by bearing in mind the following principles:

a) The minister should ordinarily have some input into the leading of worship, be it the call to worship, the intercessions, the confession or some short introductions. While this obviously does not need to happen every week, there is something amiss if several weeks go by without the person with main pastoral oversight of the congregation taking an active lead in worship. One area where it is usually better for the minister (if he or she has been the preacher) not to lead, is if there is a time of response or prayer scheduled to follow the preaching of the Word. I don't know if my experience is normative, but it is next to impossible for me really to know what parts of a sermon have spoken particularly to the congregation at large. For someone who has sat and listened to lead this time of response, seems to make sense.

b) Worship should be led, more often than not, by people who have been selected carefully, have an appropriate degree of musical knowledge and competence, and have undergone, or are undergoing theological instruction. Most churches believe in the necessity of theological training for pastors and preachers. If worship leading is a vital part of the church's life (and I have argued above that the headline worship leaders are actually the primary preachers to today's generation) then why are we so haphazard about who we get to do it? I have been concerned over the years at how sometimes gifted young musicians, but immature and uncommitted Christians, can go from fellowship to fellowship and find themselves in a short space of time up at the front leading worship, before going off in a short while to some other church (usually) with a better band. It is my conviction that those who are given the privilege of leading in worship should be evidently committed to the congregation and involved, or become involved, in some degree of pastoral care, thereby ensuring a degree of sensitivity in their leadership towards the needs and issues faced by the worshippers, and also ensuring that they have a degree of respect within the fellowship. There is much talk of worship leaders needing to be sensitive to the Holy Spirit, and rightly so, but there is also a need for a sensitivity on the human level.

c) A good leadership team will listen to one another. If the minister's knowledge of hymnology is limited, he or she must humbly defer to the opinions and advice of others on the team. Similarly, musicians and other worship leaders must listen to the advice of the minister regarding the general direction and tone of the worship, being prepared to adapt and change from their preferred styles if necessary. Leading and accompanying worship are acts of service for the whole people of God, not ego-trips or opportunities for showmanship. The balance between ministering and monopolising rests on whether or not the minister is prepared to take seriously this mentoring and advisory role, including regular review and reassessment. The lazy options are to monopolise, or abdicate altogether.

In short, one cannot overestimate the benefits of having a team of gifted people trained to share in this task: there will be variety for the congregation, a maturing of gifts for the one(s) leading, and renewal for the minister who learns what it means to be ministered to. Practically, the following steps may be necessary:

a) An identification, over time, of people of spiritual understanding who are gifted in this area, and who could be encouraged to lead in worship without resorting to cliché. Please note, an ability to play the guitar is not necessary for this role.

b) The training and equipping of such people in the basic issues of hymnology: through an exposure to the vast variety of material available; an analysis of the strengths and weaknesses of various pieces, their appropriateness to certain settings, and so on; and an experience of different styles of worship, so that the best of other traditions can be utilised from time to time.

c) Communication with the other worship leaders each week, sharing with them the theme of the service, the thrust of the sermon, the issues likely to be covered, significant events within the congregation at that time; thereby giving them as full a picture as possible of the context in which they are being asked to lead worship, and maintaining the link between worship and pastoral care, highlighted above.

d) The ongoing supervision of such worship leaders through prayer and regular evaluation, asking such questions as:

- Have the hymns and the music been congruent with the theme of the service?

- Have the musical styles reflected the broad range of tastes within the congregation, thereby enabling as many people as possible to worship through a familiar medium?

- Has the music facilitated and served the communication of the Word, or has it played an over-dominant role?

- Has there been a tangible awareness of God's presence?

- Have the minds of the congregation been stretched and their experiences of worship enriched through an exposure to a variety of material from different periods, cultures, and traditions; or have they become lazily accustomed to one favourite style?

In one church in which I was involved musically, such an evaluation was carried out weekly immediately after the morning worship. While this was probably too regular and too close for objectivity, and tended to hinder personal reflection in the aftermath of worship, the principle of evaluation is good and is one way that the minister can still take seriously his responsibility of guiding public worship while moving away from being a monopoliser.

It should be remembered that if ministers generally took seriously the leading of worship, and all its potential for encouraging spiritual growth within the congregation, some of the arguments against delegating this task would have a little credibility. The truth of the matter is, however, that many ministers spend little or no time in preparation for the leading of worship (I have even heard some colleagues refer to worship as 'the preliminaries'), therefore they have little right to complain when others do it less than perfectly.

THE NOT-SO-MERRY ORGAN

If the ability to play the guitar has been seen in some circles as a prerequisite to leading worship, in many mainline churches the organ enjoys similar status. Donald Webster is typical of many organists in that he presupposes not only their continued existence in all churches, but also their pre-eminence when it comes to music. He writes: 'The organist by virtue of his specialised knowledge, will have the lion's share of the responsibility.'[2] Yet he never justifies why this has to be so, and such justification is required since the church survived very well without organs and organists for more than a millennium, and even after they were introduced would have accompanied hymn-singing in only a minority of larger, wealthier churches for many years. Yet Webster is no more than patronisingly tolerant of other musicians playing in the service. He appears to speak favourably of the edict of Pope Pius X in 1903 which forbade instruments other than the organ except by special permission and agrees with Percy Scholes that this edict laid down principles which 'cultured, intelligent and devout musicians [recognised] as being sound'. Webster then condescends to write: 'But clearly there are occasions when other instruments may have to be used, and are being used, sometimes in an attempt to be 'with it', and these may be considered briefly'.[3] Such presumption is of little help in releasing the wide range of musical abilities within many congregations, and simply mirrors the ministerial monopolisation criticised above. The 1992 *Report of the Archbishops' Commission on Church Music* also rather complacently (and chauvenistically) presupposed that the organ will remain the most likely instrument to accompany worship for the foreseeable future.[4]

While I am appreciative of good organ music, several factors call into question its appropriateness in the modern context. Firstly, the cost of maintaining an organ has become prohibitive for a lot of congregations when there are so many

---

2   D. Webster, op. cit., p. 6.
3   Webster, op. cit., p. 49.
4   *In Tune With Heaven*, para. 600.

other needy areas where the money could be beneficially spent. I heard recently of an inner-city congregation with a mission-field of thousands on its doorstep and numerous potential outreach possibilities among the economically deprived, but who chose instead to spend £30,000 on fixing an organ for the benefit of its 100 or so members. This is surely indicative of sadly misplaced priorities.

Secondly, the organ is no longer the most appropriate form of accompaniment for a vast number of contemporary pieces. Yet the expense of the organ means that congregations feel that they need to justify having it and therefore it is either played to accompany pieces for which it is unsuited, or contemporary non-organ pieces are simply not selected. This is clearly a case of the tail wagging the dog.

Thirdly, good and well-qualified organists are not easy to find, and therefore many organs are played by pianists or other musicians who don't bring out the best in them. This dearth can lead to churches grasping at anyone with the right technical ability regardless of spirituality or suitability to the wider and more important task of leading worship. Again the financial issue tends to be the driving force. Instead of looking at what musical accompaniment is best suited to the material being sung and in line with the resources of the congregation, an organist is immediately sought on the basis that 'we need someone to play this thing'.

Fourthly, many organists, even technically good ones, can also have a control mentality when it comes to choosing and playing material. Therefore they do not choose what is outside of their particular taste and can also be prone to drowning out whatever other instruments are playing along with them.

Fifthly, like the instruments they play, organists can be expensive commodities. While, if resources and priorities permit, there is merit in paying for a full-time musical director who will co-ordinate and develop the entire musical dimension of congregational life in conjunction with the church leadership, the practice of paying thousands to the organist, when other instrumentalists and singers are participating voluntarily, is somewhat unfair. If the organ is to be used (and I'm not advocating its total demise) it must take its place alongside the other instruments and the organist must be treated on an equal footing with other musicians.

While many salaried full-time and part-time organists and musical directors have played a vital role in revitalising the praise of congregations, it may be erroneously assumed that unless one has the financial resources to pay for a full-time musical director, little can be done in this area. This is not the case. I remember preaching in a church which had an above-average choral group, and a very competent band incorporating percussion, guitars, string, woodwind and keyboard, but where none of the musicians were paid. Rather, the leading and co-ordination of the music was shared around a team of volunteers. This resulted in a lively and varied repertoire that would have been the envy of many churches with salaried musicians.

Finally, in some missionary situations it is possible that, for all its many qualities, the organ still carries negative connotations of 'church' for many whom we are seeking to reach, and this is something that must be borne in mind. It could be argued that this is the case in most situations—not just 'missionary' ones. A recent survey in North America found that less than 4% of the population listened to classical music, and less than half of those appreciated organ music. Yet the organ still dominates most churches. If the music to which our people listen from day to day is orchestral, or electric-based rock, or acoustic folk, then the case for the dominance of the organ totally disappears, particularly since there is such a wide variety of good material available for performance by the other media.

In order to conclude this issue on a positive note, there is something to be said for one or two churches in a given region maintaining a good organ so that, in those places and at special regional events, the undeniable benefits of a Bach chorale or an improvised organ accompaniment to a hymn tune can be enjoyed by all. This way, those who wish can still experience the grandeur and majesty of the organ, while the majority of congregations are freed to explore alternative options.

SWEET SINGING IN THE CHOIR?

Another source of potential conflict is the choir. Much of what has been written above regarding the organist, could apply equally here. Choirs exist not to dictate, nor to dominate, the praise. In some situations they need not exist at all. In fact, in churches where eight or nine people continue to exist as a sad relic of former glory-days, they would be better to disband and seek a totally new approach. Nevertheless, if they exist (and I believe they can still play a role) they should do so to perform appropriate choral music as a part of worship. There is something therefore to be said for choirs existing ad hoc, to practise and perform suitable material for particular occasions, and the rest of the time to sit and worship with the main body. Later we will look at John Bell's 'Ten Golden Rules for teaching new songs'; one of these states that if the choir are expected to lead the congregation in song, there can be an advantage in positioning them behind or among the people rather than at the front. In one Presbyterian congregation I attended, I often felt that the congregational singing was better on Communion Sundays when the choir was dispersed among the people.

I believe that many of the conflicts surrounding choirs are not helped by their existence as a permanent body (lobby?) sometimes robed, and often seated in a prominent part of the building. Although Webster[5] argues against anthems being a sop to the choir's vanity, this is actually a very good description of what many anthems have become. Surely it would be much healthier if, in the same way as the organ takes its place alongside other instruments, the choir were to take their place alongside other forms of vocal leadership, appearing and disappearing as required. This would have the added advantage of allowing some people to be members of different groups and the long-standing problem of getting singers to be committed to a choir may be solved in some measure.

This brings us to the important difference between performance music and congregational music. Both have their place, and there is no reason why 'performance music' cannot

---

5   Op. cit., p. 5.

take a variety of forms. In one church in which I worked, 'anthems' were successfully performed by a variety of groups: senior choir, children's choir, solos, an adult-orientated rock band, youth worship group, a capella group, organ, and small orchestra. Other places may be able to supplement this with folk music, string quartets, jazz or blues ensemble, different shades of rock/pop, or mellow acoustic ballads with interpretative dance, to name but a few. The creative possibilities are legion and each has something to offer. Although there is a difference in function between music in which the congregation joins, and music to which they listen, there is no reason why both cannot be an edifying part of worship.

Chapter 8

Spoilt for Choice?

What conclusions can we come to regarding the type of material which is to be sung? I have argued for a sensible balance of old and new, and I would also advocate a variety of styles and a healthy combination of formal liturgy and open spontaneity. These need not all be present in a single service, but a congregation that can comfortably embrace such variety has a lot going for it.

INAPPROPRIATE STYLES?

The question of appropriateness of style has never disappeared: polyphony, folk, Bach's *Passions*, parlour songs, music-hall, jazz, and rock have all in their turn been condemned by traditionalists as 'inappropriate'. It is fascinating to realise that in the time of J. S. Bach, one of the criteria for employing church musicians was that they 'adhere to the modern fashionable...style, so that congregations would be able to hear both the old and the new, and both tastes would be pleased'.[1] Yet Bach faced much opposition in doing this, and never expected his music to be any more durable than that of his contemporaries. It is also interesting to notice that some of his choral music had its roots in the dance music of the day with its strong beat and 'walking bass', and was often an adaptation of dance motifs which he had composed for the Royal Court.

Because of the swiftness of cultural change it is often difficult for us to appreciate the significance of these debates of past eras. Nevertheless, we can see a contemporary example in

---

1   Wilson-Dickson, op. cit., p. 88.

the various attitudes to pop/rock in worship. It is amazing how most of the writers on worship are at least cautious about its use. Some like Routley[2] are writing too early in the development of rock, when it could still be dismissed as a passing fad. But others like Dean[3] attempt to articulate reasons for their reticence, and in so doing are unconvincing and contradictory.

These are some of the problems he highlights: rock music is easy to consume, entertainment-orientated, it contains elements of Romanticism, and is inhospitable to quality. But Dean has spent a large part of his book defending the 'Gospel-song' as a serious music-form in its own right, yet all these things (even if they were true) could be said of that genre. This is even more evident when he tries to be specific in his criticism of rock: 'The overpowering beat is static, hypnotic and without counterpoint or anticipated harmonic or melodic progression.' In addition, he highlights rock's success-orientation, capitalisation on sensationalism and its transience. But none of these are essential qualities of rock music and, it could be argued, can be redeemed in the right context.

He then switches his attention to the 'associations' of rock, its 'crude and vulgar lyrics', and the lifestyle of many of its headliners. What betrays this argument is that it is an argument from an 'outsider'—one who has not grown up in, nor understands, the rock culture of today. For him, the genre carries those connotations, for that is his limited experience of it. But for others those are not connotations which are implicit within the musical form itself. For many today, it is quite easy to differentiate between wholesome and unwholesome rock in the same manner as they evaluate any other aspect of the media. Frame tackles critics such as Marva Dawn and D. G. Hart on this same issue and urges them to become a little more familiar with the music they are criticising[4] before

---

2   In *Twentieth Century Church Music* (1964).

3   Dean, op. cit., pp. 256-60.

4   Frame, *Contemporary Worship Music*, *passim*, see especially pp. 84, 121. He spends a good deal of time interacting with Marva Dawn's *Reaching out without Dumbing Down*, Grand Rapids: Eerdmans, 1995; and D. G.

issuing generalised condemnations and even slanderous accusations.[5]

Critics who don't understand the pop/rock idiom or dismiss it all out of hand, choose to ignore the fact that traditional churches are emptying and many are going to alternative fellowships where the contemporary style is exclusively employed. Furthermore, it is no longer possible to say that the rock medium is being used simply to be trendy or to try to appeal to people outside the church, because since the 1980s a good percentage of contemporary Christian music has been written by people who have not had traditional church upbringings, but who have come to faith and are expressing their faith in the musical idiom with which they feel comfortable. The Archbishops' Report highlighted this, and the resulting tension it can cause, but didn't go very far along the road towards resolving it.

> Quite a number of musicians who are at home in the 'renewal' idiom have grown up outside the church. Whilst they bring a welcome freshness and enthusiasm to worship, they may also lack a sympathetic understanding of the Church's liturgy and tradition. Moreover, for home-produced music and self-taught instrumental playing, the only role models for many young vocalists and groups are provided through television and pop concerts. It is not therefore surprising if there is sometimes an over-provision of microphones and electronic equipment and a prevalence of noise, not least the persistent beat of a drum-kit.

> Sensitive guidance may be needed for young musicians. Without in any way discouraging them, they may need advice on providing music for worship which is acceptable to the many different people in a congregation. There is an ever-growing amount of musical material in this genre and musicians and clergy need to be wise and selective in their choice of it. Skill is also required to arrange it for a particular choir, group or instruments.[6]

There is an element of patronisation here in 'home-produced music and self-taught instrumental playing'. It is clear that

---

Hart, 'Post-modern Evangelical Worship', *Calvin Theological Journal* 30 (1995), pp. 451-9.

[5] See ibid., pp. 79-80, 113.

[6] *In Tune with Heaven*, paras 629-30.

electronic equipment and drum-kits are barely tolerated. It is not, of course, just with regard to renewal music that there is a wide selection to choose from, or that care is needed in the choice. Nor is the fact that television and pop-concerts constitute the musical role model for young people necessarily any more problematic than when it was the Baroque concert-hall and Victorian music-hall. More serious though is the suggestion that what is paramount is that music be provided 'which is acceptable to the many different people in a congregation'. Surely what is biblically faithful, doctrinally helpful, God-honouring and culturally rooted is what should govern our choice rather than congregational acceptance. All in all, the Archbishops' report is a fair indicator of the breadth of styles currently used in churches and, in the true nature of church reports, limits itself to description and generalisations and carefully balanced suggestions. Cynically one could say it pleases no-one and offends no-one.

Some commentators are often too ready to tar all rock musicians with the same brush, regarding all their compositions as insubstantial and transient, evidently unaware of the complexities and counterpoint that typify the best practitioners and the 'classics' of rock that have outlived their own generation. To impose an entire value system onto an art genre is a quantum leap unworthy of serious critics, but it is a common one among traditional Christian musicians who view the rock world 'from outside'. They also forget that the Elizabethan madrigals of Morley et al. contained some risqué lyrics, and the lifestyle of many classical composers (including those whose music is played regularly as organ offertories and postludes in our churches) was far from virtuous.

No, 'associations' are very subjective. For, as pointed out in the introduction to this book, many in contemporary society associate Victorian hymns with tiresome Sunday School classes, or dusty school Assembly halls. Personal traumas connected with strict upbringings or strongly disciplinarian religious schools could mean that these hymns have more harmful associations for the unbeliever or new Christian than any rock song. My point is not to be uncritical of rock, or hold it up as the best or only contemporary medium for worship, but to defend its right to be used in the correct context. Wilson-Dickson acknowledges that 'all of rock's most resilient features, the beat, the drama, the group vibrations derive from Gospel', but the big danger is commercialisation: 'To move gospel music out of the church and into the world of entertainment,' he writes, 'changes it subtly,' for the musical and emotional has been exploited while the spiritual has been denied or perverted.[7] This is a valid point and one that I would share particularly with regard to the recent 'worship explosion', whereby a number of the contemporary worship leaders whose work is critiqued in the earlier chapters are under increasing pressure to release CDs and embark on 'worship concert tours'. Worship is now big business. Whatever the dangers of the commercialisation of Christian performance pop, the commercialisation of Christian worship music is sailing perilously close to the winds of materialistic idolatry.

Nevertheless this is a separate issue.[8] The commercially-driven production of certain music and the artificially created demand for it says nothing about its acceptability or otherwise as a valid medium for worship. I believe we must be prepared to shelve any remaining qualms we have about the appropriateness of certain musical genres within worship. Tallis has his place, Sankey has his place, Kendrick has his and the electric guitars have theirs. Only when we get beyond the futile wranglings of the past which have centred on the inherent evil of rock, for example, can we make more mature and informed decisions about the suitability, not of genres, but of particular pieces for our public worship.

Unfortunately, common sense does not always reign on this issue, and the passage of time seems to have done little to bring the various camps closer together. Frame refers to the problem of musical snobbery, and is forthright in condemning it as sin:

> One kind of sin...is musical snobbery. Sometimes music leaves us cold
> because we are too stubborn to open ourselves to a style different from

---

[7]   Op. cit., p. 203.

[8]   See Frame, *Contemporary Worship Music*, chapter 6.

what we are used to. Snobs are of many types: high art lovers who cannot bear to hear anything from mere popular culture, but also 'with it' modern types who look down on others for being less than fully up-to-date. Such snobbery is, more evidently than the problem of a lack of education, one that God has called his church to deal with.[9]

At a later point in his book he writes with bemusement of those rigorous academics who seem to lose hold of their discipline and allow their emotions to take over when they venture to deal with the subject of contemporary worship music:

> Why this remarkable carelessness in research and argumentation from people who are ordinarily intelligent and balanced in their theological judgment? And why do the critics approach Contemporary Worship Music in such a shrill tone? Even if their arguments were somewhat better, would it not be more appropriate for them to gently urge the young songwriters to move in better directions, rather than to dismiss the entire movement as worthless? One suspects that the critics' problems with Contemporary Worship Music are not merely theological, but personal, even emotional. It seems that they *just don't like* Contemporary Worship Music, and they are searching for reasons (however inadequate those reasons may be to an objective reader) to justify that dislike.[10]

He concludes:

> Much of what I have been saying may fall on deaf ears because the traditionalist opposition to Contemporary Worship Music is, in my judgment, not wholly based on theology. There is a large emotional component to it. I know of no other way to explain the shoddy argumentation and the sheer stubborness of the Contemporary Worship Music critics.... My response to the emotional problems of those facing the loss, or partial loss, of tradition [is that] God wants us to count all things but loss for the sake of Christ. That works both ways, of course. Both those who love traditional hymns and those who love the new songs need to be flexible, to understand one another and minister to one another. What we must not do is to lash out at one another with false pretensions to knowledge, sophistication, and rationality, and with intellectual arguments that are little more than masks for underlying anger.[11]

---

9   Ibid., pp. 19–20.
10 Ibid., pp. 129–30.
11 Ibid., pp. 142–3.

I heartily agree with Frame's analysis here, for if we are to contribute to the new church landscape nationwide through reintroducing some of the wealth of the hymnody of the past we will only be heard if we are both tolerant of, and conversant with, the best of the new.

GENDER INCLUSIVENESS

We turn now to an issue which has arisen in the last couple of decades and which is affecting hymnology and vexing hymn-book compilers for the first time. For many women in our churches, especially those coming new into our fellowships, using male pronouns to encompass the whole of humanity creates unnecessary barriers and may foster feelings of alienation. They feel excluded from, and therefore have difficulty singing, hymns which use the generic 'man'. Whether or not this is solely as a result of a radical feminist agenda, or an example of linguistic change, is a moot point. Even if it is the former, it should not prevent us from taking seriously the concerns raised. When referring to humanity, the male pronoun 'he', and the biblical 'man' (Hebrew *adam,* or *ish*; Greek *anthropos*) in many contexts clearly includes female.[12] So changing our vocabulary to express this is simply good sense, another example of cultural contextualisation where no doctrinal principle is at stake. Contrasting views on headship, patriarchy and male leadership in the church are unaffected by this change; traditionalists and radicals, conservatives and liberals alike, should feel comfortable with such gender inclusiveness. Even if we do feel uncomfortable, if we have an evangelistic heart, that heart should include feminists, and therefore any change which makes it easier for them to hear the Word of God and to worship should be welcomed.

12　See M. L. Strauss, *Distorting Scripture? The Challenge of Bible Translation and Gender Accuracy*, Downers Grove: IVP, 1998, pp. 103ff.; appendix 2.

Webster, like many purists, opposes the modernisation of lyrics,[13] but he is writing in 1983 before the gender issue became so prominent. Besides, once hymns are seen not as sacrosanct poetry (which Webster seems to be advocating) but as flexible vehicles for worship, the case against modifications is substantially weakened. Already some hymn books have engaged in gender-sensitive revision. The new Canadian Presbyterian *Book of Praise* (1996) is 'moderately' inclusive in that human references are all inclusive, and God is often referred to as 'he', but sometimes the compilers have switched to the second person or simply inserted the word 'God'. Examples include:

> Praise to the Lord, the Almighty, who rules all creation:
> My soul, praise God who alone is your health and salvation.
> Come, all who hear, sisters and brothers draw near,
> Joining in glad adoration.[14]

Notice the inversion of the usual order in 'sisters and brothers', and how the alteration of the second line from the original 'O my soul praise him', actually puts the vocal stress on the object 'God' rather than the verb 'praise'.

While consistently replacing 'He' with 'God' could run the risk of reducing a personal living God to an abstract concept, 'God is love: let heaven adore him' is a good example of a hymn that has been strengthened poetically by having more references to 'God', instead of pronouns:

> God is love: come heaven adoring,
> God is love: come earth rejoice.
> Come creation, voices soaring,
> Sing exulting with one voice.
> God who laid the earth's foundation,
> God who spread the heavens above.
> God who breathes through all creation,
> God is love, eternal love.[15]

---

13   Op. cit., p. 53ff.
14   *The Book of Praise*, Toronto: PCC, 1996, no. 321.
15   No. 314

In 'Hark the herald angels sing',[16] 'Pleased as man with man to dwell' has become 'Pleased on earth with us to dwell'. Jubilate Hymns' *Carol Praise*,[17] have opted for the middle ground on this one, changing only the human reference 'Pleased as man with us to dwell.'

This issue has also exercised Bible translators in recent years. In the conclusion to his excellent book *Distorting Scripture? The Challenge of Bible Translation and Gender Accuracy*[18] Mark Strauss (himself a traditionalist or 'complementarian' in terms of male and female roles within the church) asks for rationality and what he terms 'gender-accuracy': that is, to translate inclusively all instances where the original language meant to be inclusive.

> While complementarians and egalitarians may disagree over whether [Galatians 3:28] is intended to eliminate distinct roles for men or women in the church and the home, there is one point on which we can all certainly agree: Paul is here stressing the *full inclusion* of men and women in the gift of salvation provided through Jesus Christ. If we ask which translation, 'a *man* is justified by faith' (Romans 3:28 NIV) or 'a *person* is justified by faith (NIV Inclusive Version), brings out *better* the inclusive sense so central to this apostolic gospel, the answer appears to me to be obvious.[19]

He makes a plea that we do not allow this issue to be governed by competing social and political agendas, but that we employ the tried and tested rules of translation theory, in the interest of proper communication. I would make the same plea with regard to hymnody.

The issue becomes more controversial when we leave the realm of human gender and deal with masculine references for God. Here the case for change is not so strong. The alternatives are to refer to God in terms of function: 'Creator', 'Ruler', etc.; or title: 'the Lord', or simply 'God'; or even with alternating masculine and feminine pronouns. However, these either reduce God from 'person' to functionary, concentrating

---

16   No. 139
17   Basingstoke: Marshall Pickering, 1987, no. 115.
18   Downers Grove: IVP, 1998.
19   Ibid., p. 204.

on what he does rather than who he is, or in the case of the feminine pronouns, go further than Scripture itself is willing to go. Of course God is supra–gender, male and female are made in his image, and feminine metaphors are used of him, but it is significant that Scripture while acknowledging all of the above, still refers to 'him'. All attempts to change or dilute this run the danger of undermining the personhood of God. It is important that this is safeguarded, particularly in worship.

Some point to the feminine gender of the Hebrew word for Spirit *ruach*, to justify using feminine pronouns, but Hebrew grammarians have pointed out that the gender classification has nothing to do with sex, but is simply a linguistic convenience by which different groups of words are categorised.[20] It is also worth pointing out that whereas *ruach* primarily refers to 'wind', the doctrine of the Spirit is much more fully developed in the New Testament where the word *pneuma* is actually neuter (although, interestingly, it defies the rules of grammar by taking a masculine pronoun).

OLD AND NEW

The natural human propensity to gravitate towards that which we like, or that with which we are familiar, has meant that most of our worship services are unbalanced. Let me state again: living in the late twentieth century, we have available to us a wealth of instrumental, choral and hymnic material unparalleled in any other era. Laziness and a narrow musical focus have led ministers and worship leaders to choose the majority of material from a short list of 'favourites' and the 'performance music' tends to be of one style only. Wilson-Dickson moans: 'if only Evangelicals...could feel happy singing Byrd and Gibbons as well as Graham Kendrick';[21] while

---

[20] See B. K. Waltke and M. O'Connor, *An Introduction to Biblical Hebrew Syntax*, Winona Lake: Eisenbrauns, 1990, chapter 6. See especially pp. 99-102 where examples are given from ancient and modern languages of male animates which are classified as 'feminine'. See also S. E. Porter, *Idioms of the Greek New Testament (2nd ed.)*, Sheffield: JSOT Press, 1994, pp. 100-102.

[21] Wilson-Dickson, op. cit., p. 7.

Hustad remarks: 'for many evangelical groups...serious hymn singing is little more than "tokenism".... Many congregations repeat the same ten or fifteen or twenty hymns over and over, Sunday after Sunday.'[22]

Some have reckoned that congregations have a repertoire of only 100 hymns a year.[23] I think this is an optimistic estimate, and the situation deteriorates considerably when one leaves the milieu of mainline churches, and examines the hymn diet of wider Evangelicalism. The conservatism of the church in hymn singing is graphically illustrated in that Hustad's list of the 'top twenty' contains all those listed by Dean as favourites 'across-the board' at the turn of the century. Dean's list is as follows: 1. All Hail the Power; 2. Come, Thou Almighty King; 3. Holy, Holy, Holy; 4. O for a thousand tongues to sing; 5. Love Divine; 6. O Worship the King; 7. Crown Him with many crowns; 8. Faith of our Fathers; 9. O God, our help in ages past; 10. Come Thou Fount of every blessing. [24]

What is particularly significant, though, is that I found that six of these ten (all except 2, 6, 8, 9), plus perhaps 'And Can it Be', 'Be thou my Vision' and 'When I survey', account for the sum total of older hymns sung at a late twentieth-century international graduate theological seminary over a period of three years. If the hymn diet of those being prepared for pastoral ministry worldwide is limited to nine pieces from the previous centuries then it is no wonder that the evangelical church is indeed impoverished in this area. It seems that there is now the belief that the only material worth learning is new material. Webster makes the valid comment that 'the timeless classics are permanently contemporary'.[25]

Of course a thoughtless lumping together of songs from different eras, simply to achieve a balance, would be ludicrous and miss the whole point of worship, resulting in nothing more than a clever post-modern musical montage.

---

[22] D. Hustad, *Jubilate! Church Music in the Evangelical Tradition*, Carol Stream: Hope, 1981, p. 255. Webster, op. cit., p. 10.

[23] Webster, op. cit., p. 10.

[24] Op. cit., pp. 59-60.

[25] Webster, op. cit., p. 8.

Nevertheless, there is no reason why the following contrasting styles could not be utilised from time to time by most churches.[26]

Plainsong melody, Taizé chant, Iona 'world music', instrumental or vocal solo:- as a call to worship (meditative), or as a response to prayers of confession or intercession.

Organ chorale, orchestral or mellow band instrumental:- as a call to worship (meditative), or to accompany or follow the reading of Scripture.

Jazz or rock instrumental, organ fugue, brass fanfare:- as call to worship (celebratory) or postlude (celebratory).

A choral, folk or rock anthem:- to be performed according to theme and at relevant point in service.

Traditional hymn-form:- to be sung by all and drawn from all periods: Psalms, pre-Reformation, Reformation, Wesleyan, Victorian, early 20th century, Hymns for Today's Church, Iona.

Informal medleys:- a pooling together of appropriate worship material, incorporating contemporary worship songs, gospel-song refrains, even fragments of hymns, to be sung by all.

It is of course vital that whoever has the responsibility for choosing the material has access to the necessary resources, and also that, over time, they become acquainted with the riches of the past, adept at rediscovering forgotten 'treasures', alert to current developments within worship music, aware of the global scene, and willing to learn by exposing themselves to hitherto unfamiliar worship styles. Since one person's musical knowledge and taste will be limited, a pool of people with differing musical tastes could meet regularly with the minister and/or musical director and assist them by offering suggestions of potential 'anthems' of relevance to the theme.

---

26   For some examples of the following see Appendix.

LOCAL AND GLOBAL

We should not be hesitant in encouraging song-writing gifts to blossom within our local contexts. If, in our churches, we encourage prayer in the words of the people, evangelism in the words of the people, testimony in the words of the people; and if we aim for preaching that is not only biblical but contemporary and rooted in the local situation, why not occasionally encourage the people's praise to be in their own words and born out of the existential circumstances facing that congregation at that time?

I can think of several occasions where a recently-composed song has been used to great effect within the composer's local congregation. It was often lyrically unpolished, musically unexciting, and would be unlikely to find a place in any published anthology for the use of the wider church (although, judging by the standard of some published material critiqued earlier, this is probably a reflection more on the vagaries of the Christian music publishing industry than on the inherent quality of the piece). On each occasion the piece's appropriateness and integrity stemmed from the relationship between composer and local congregation. Here was someone the people knew and respected, and who knew and respected the people. There was an irreproducable dynamic which meant that what would have been discarded as second-rate elsewhere had a validity and a positive ministry in that one local situation, in much the same way that stuttering, repetitive, ungrammatical extempore prayers may touch the heart in a local service, but would not be preserved and published in a liturgical collection. This connects again with the pastoral dimension of worship-leading mentioned earlier.

Just as we should not allow published anthologies to stifle hymn-writing talent within our congregations, neither should we allow them to close our eyes to much of the useful praise material which is available from other cultures. Fortunately a number of recent song-books have sought to include pieces from the world church. A look at the contents of *Songs of God's People* (1988), *Let's Praise* (1988, 1994), *Rejoice and Sing*

(1991), *Glory to God* (1994) and *Common Ground* (1998),[27] shows an increasing respect for, and the increasing popularity of, Christian 'world music'. In addition there have been collections such as *Many and Great*,[28] which have been comprised entirely of short liturgical responses and worship songs from the four corners of the globe. These pieces can quite easily be fitted in to services at a variety of points: as invocations, intercessions, responses, benedictions or amens, in much the same way as the Taizé pieces have already been incorporated into some Protestant churches for many years. Although the Taizé material is almost exclusively based on pieces from the Latin liturgy, some of the translations can be used in reformed and non-conformist circles. 'Laudate omnes gentes', for example, can be a beautiful call to worship using the words: 'Sing praises, all you people; Sing praises to the Lord.' Similarly, 'O Lord, hear our prayer' is suitable for introducing prayers or interspersing between intercessions.[29]

In terms of other 'world music', the South African 'Thu ma mina'[30] is a suitable response to prayer, as is the Argentinian 'Sanctus',[31] and the Peruvian 'Gloria'[32] makes an excellent and lively call to worship. 'Mayenziwe',[33] also from South Africa is wonderful in between intercessions. For a lively alternative to the dirges of squawked choral Amens still

---

27 *Songs of God's People*, Oxford: OUP, 1988 (Church of Scotland); *Let's Praise 1, 2*, London: Marshall Pickering, 1988, 1994 (English cross-denominational but mainly Anglican); *Rejoice and Sing*, Oxford: OUP, 1991 (English, United Reformed Church); *Glory to God*, Oxford: OUP, 1994 (Presbyterian Church in Ireland); and *Common Ground*, Edinburgh: St Andrew Press, 1998 (Scottish, ecumenical).

28 Glasgow: Wild Goose Publications, 1990.

29 The Taizé music is quite well represented (although curiously without translations that can be fitted into the music) in *Rejoice and Sing*.

30 *Songs of God's People*, no. 108; *Common Ground*, no. 129. Bell's 'We will lay our burden down' *Love From Below*, p. 82, is also very effective in this regard.

31 *Common Ground*, no. 48.

32 *Common Ground*, no. 101.

33 *Common Ground*, no. 84.

surviving in too many churches, try another South African tune 'Amen siyakudumisa'.[34] This is great as a recessional.

ENDURING AND TRANSIENT

Analysing hymns for their musical and literary content, as we did above, is useful in that we want to offer our best to God, and if certain musical and poetic devices can be used to facilitate worship, then it is important to know what they are. However, such analyses have their limitations. Wilson-Dickson points out that what is good for music may be bad for worship. He writes: 'Enthusiastic congregational singing, which arises from positive spiritual commitment, may be a dimension far more important than the musical idiom.'[35] Manwaring claims that the best hymns are good poetry but he also admits that 'some well-loved hymns are poor poetry but...we do not despise them on that account. They have their ministry.' He continues: 'How many of our modern repetitive unstructured songs will survive into the 21st century? Yet, as they have a place in our worship to-day, does that really matter?'[36]

If many of the pieces used in our worship services are less than excellent, should they therefore be jettisoned altogether? Is their popularity and usefulness within the contemporary church a sign that they have a right to be there, or a sign that the church culture needs to be renewed? I think the solution lies in taking their popularity seriously while, at the same time, never being satisfied with simply deferring to popular taste. The popularity of contemporary worship music is surely indicative of a feeling that technical quality is not everything, and that the pursuit of pure artistic and musical excellence for its own sake is an unproductive and arid cul-de-sac.

The crucial difference between what is a perfectly healthy sign of variety within the people of God, and what is a cause for great concern, is between mediocre hymns being *present* in

---

34   *Common Ground*, no. 7.
35   Wilson-Dickson, op. cit., pp. 243-4.
36   Manwaring, op. cit., pp. ix-x.

the worship, and their *characterising* the worship. I don't believe that there are sufficient theological, philosophical or methodological grounds for denying them their place, but the reasons for limiting, restricting, or balancing their use are multitudinous.

This brings us to Routley's interesting concept of 'expendable' music. Routley is at heart a traditionalist, but he acknowledges that in admitting informal and perhaps locally written material to our worship, we are doing something refreshingly new.

> There is a place in church music for what is impermanent.... The church might well explore the possibilities of 'local' music, and of material which because of its emergence from a genuine local situation could make a decisive impact once without being such as would make any impact at all on any repetition. Certainly, if this were considered seriously by a church group, the chances of getting some of the rust off the joints of that local enterprise, which in folksong days was the very life of the nation's music, become a little less dim than they are at present.[37]

Webster rejects this 'planned obsolescence theory'. He writes: 'For us to bother with the ephemeral, knowing it to be so, is a waste of time and talents'.[38] This is a value judgment without any firm basis. Since most of what we do and enjoy in life is transient, durability is a relative concept. Surely the Spirit can move us to worship through a hymn which we may never use or require again?

As mentioned above, grass-roots informal material can have a very important function in the life of a congregation. For a start, such pieces have the added advantage of being the response of today's church facing today's issues and therefore they have a place in today's, if not tomorrow's, worship. The problem arises when the right to posterity is presumed and the church is inundated with reams of newly published material. As well as fanning the fires of commercialism and elevating this stuff to a status higher than it deserves, such mass-production actively stifles local talent and prevents the release of potentially rewarding gifts from within the Body.

---

37   E. Routley, *20th Century Church Music*, p. 193.
38   Op. cit., p. 22.

Devotional and Didactic

We are to worship with heart and mind. Many of the debates and conflicts regarding worship can be traced to an overemphasis of one or the other. Yet both must be engaged as we seek to meet with God. There needs to be a moving of the heart, and there is a place for pieces, usually in the form of short devotional phrases, through which we simply express our love for and commitment to our Lord.

Nevertheless, this devotion is more likely to be genuine and lasting if our minds have first been engaged and we have considered exactly what God has done for us in Christ. We cannot forget the didactic role of hymnody. From the days of Ambrose, through Luther and Wesley, what was sung was the doctrine of the church. We are losing this, and losing it rapidly. Our people today are more literate, supposedly better educated and have more theological resources at their fingertips than their ancestors had. Yet too often we content ourselves with singing material that has not a fraction of the depth of a Wesley hymn which was used to instruct the English labourers of the eighteenth century. On several occasions already I have upheld the value of the informal, devotional and contemporary, but two of Dean's questions still stand and still need to be heard. He asks: 'Will our less cerebral and more experience-orientated music have a long-term debilitating effect upon the spiritual and musical life of the believing community?' and 'Is the church abdicating its role to teach the music of witness and worship to meet the total ministry of the church for all of its people?'[39]

The songs we sing from day to day have a powerful effect on our minds and memories. My grandfather was 97 years old when he died. In his later years when he could no longer read or attend church, he fed himself on the words of hymns and psalms he had stored up through decades of singing. If all that we and our children have sung is variations on the theme of 'Jesus, I love you'—structureless, unmemorable songs which came into our lives for a few months and left quickly—we may reach an age when we can learn no new words, and when

---

[39] Dean, op. cit., pp. 255-6.

we vainly reach out for something durable and substantial to remind us of the ground on which our love for Jesus was based.

Chapter 9

The Task in Hand

LEADING

There is an extent to which the leading of worship cannot be taught, and is dependent upon such immeasurable factors as the leader's current spiritual walk with God and, less importantly, the personalities and dynamics within and between the leadership and worship teams. Nevertheless, the following guidelines may be found to be helpful.

Pitfalls to Avoid

a) Too much talking: the temptation will always be to justify our existence at the front by saying a lot. This can be debilitating rather than helpful in worship. Sometimes such introductions turn into mini-sermons, on other occasions they simply repeat what the song is saying (and saying much better), at other times they become repetitive and empty. Without being unkind, this is best typified by what I'll refer to as the 'Youth Fellowship worship leader', and runs something like this:

> Right, this next song is called 'Majesty' and it's really just about how majestic God is, and how we should worship him because he's done so much for us, like. And all we can do is really just exalt him, and lift up on high the name of Jesus, 'cos that's what we really want to see happen. So, like, just try to mean the words as you sing this—I know it's a really old song and all, but it's still true, and that's all I really want to say about it.
>
> (Sing 'Majesty')

> Right, this next song is called 'Rejoice, Rejoice', and it really reminds us what God wants us to do, which is just to rejoice...

This is fine for a Youth Fellowship and is probably a vital way of getting young people to take responsibility and become familiar with speaking in front of others about their faith, but too much of that in a regular Sunday service would be tiresome to say the least. The time we spend together in worship is limited and precious, therefore words must be chosen carefully.

b) No thematic connection: here, songs are chosen because of their tune, their familiarity, their popularity, rather than because of their usefulness in focussing the worshippers' hearts and minds on a particular aspect of God. Not all songs chosen, of course, need to be on the same theme. There is a place for general hymns of praise or songs of response at, for example, the opening and closing of a service, but to have no thematic thread running through a number of the songs will leave the worshippers disorientated, and opportunities will have been missed to supplement the message of the preaching through a careful choice of material. Michael Perry's compendium *Preparing for Worship: the Essential Handbook for Worship Leaders*, is almost indispensible in this regard. It is obviously limited by its date of publication, but its comprehensive indexes covering more than 200 pages (including the best scriptural index I have come across anywhere) make it a valuable starting place when it comes to selecting praise items.[1]

c) An imbalance of focus: this occurs when all the material has been of one particular orientation. Either it has been all facts *about* God, rather than worship *to* God, or it has been all about our relationship *with* God and what God is going to do *for* us, without any adoration of who God is and what he has done. A good worship leader will allow time for declaring the glory of God, as well as delighting in our relationship with him.

---

[1]   London: Marshall Pickering, 1995. Perry was also a significant contributor to, and co-editor of, *Hymns for Today's Church*.

d) Not enough time to respond: the temptation here is to fill the allotted time with scheduled songs or talking. As I mention below, we should not be afraid of silence. This is one way to get over the problem mentioned earlier of how the theology and power of so many good hymns pass us by because we sing them once and then move straight on to the next part of the service. Good worship leading will allow time to respond not only to the preaching of the Word but, on occasions, also to the reading of the Word, to a musical offering, or to a sung hymn. This response could take the form of silent prayer or guided reflection, perhaps on the words of the hymn just sung. Why for example is it only contemporary worship songs that we repeat during a service?

Some Positive Guidelines

a) In preparation, think beyond the 'play-list': leading in worship is about more than selecting and introducing songs. If suitable prayers can be prepared in advance, do so. Have some idea of the journey the worshippers will have taken in their knowledge and experience of God from the beginning to the end of the service. What questions may be in their mind at the start? What issues are some of them facing? How will the worship service have enabled them to deal with these questions and issues? Personal prayer is of course a vital aspect of this preparation.

b) Use short devotional pieces creatively; as calls to worship, or responses to longer hymns, or to break up the intercessions. If certain songs link well together, this needs to be thought out in advance and note taken not just of the musical transition but of whether or not the songs blend well in terms of message and theme.

c) Speak only when something needs to be said that hasn't already been covered by the song, or on occasions recite some of the lyrics prayerfully to embed them in the worshippers' minds. Introductions to songs should be just that, not commentaries or series of unconnected personal anecdotes.

Like a good referee at a football match, a good worship leader should not be noticed.

d) Where an introduction of more than a couple of sentences is planned, this is best scripted. Even if it is not read during the service (and it probably shouldn't be) the act of scripting will have helped in the careful choice of words.

e) Be silent rather than resort to cliché. Silence can be used creatively and does not necessarily need to be limited to times of prayer.

f) Use liturgical and pre-composed prayers as well as extempore ones. Extempore prayer is a vital part of Spirit-led reformed worship and has always been so, but there are also a wealth of prayers in the archives of church history; insights into the spiritual lives of the saints, from which we can learn much. If we are happy to sing their words in hymnody, we should not be afraid to pray their words in public worship also.

Pre-composed prayers are also a useful resource. They provide us with the opportunity to reflect at leisure on some aspect of the service's theme and draft a carefully-worded prayer which can be of great benefit to the wider congregation, particularly if they do not sound as if they are being read. This exercise is no less Spirit-led than extempore prayer and the poetry and cadences of such prayers can be used by God in the same way as skilful hymn-writing speaks to the heart.

g) Allow time for the unexpected. Our services should not be so scheduled as to crowd out God. Moments of silence, the freedom to change a song at the last moment, to allow for open prayer, or even to close the service prematurely and allow folks to respond privately, are just some ways in which we can adapt our preparation and recognise that this is no ordinary event in which we are participating. We are dealing with coming into the presence of the transcendent, unpredictable God. We do not know what he has in store for us. As worship leaders it is our job simply to create the environment in which we and the rest of God's people can meet with him and be changed by him. Sometimes something visible and tangible may occur, sometimes it may not. Nevertheless, by allowing time for the unexpected we can be sure that we have given God his place not just in our preparation, but also in the actual leading, and we will be able to tell that he has indeed been among us.

TEACHING

John Bell, as well as being a talented modern hymnwriter, has done much to equip congregations in integrating new songs into worship. A strong promoter of participation (rather than performance) in worship, his travelling workshops have been of benefit to many within the church. While Kingsway, Soul Survivor and others from within the charismatic milieu lay on regular worship workshops, these tend to be almost exclusively for musicians and ministers/leaders. This adds to the perception that a competent band is almost a pre-requisite for good worship. Bell is much more democratic and seeks to equip the whole people of God in this area. His emphasis therefore is on communal, often unaccompanied, singing. His 'Ten Golden Rules for teaching new songs'[2] are worth looking at in detail and are summarised below.

1. Believe in the voice God has given you.

2. Believe in the voice God has given other people. Years of being told, and telling themselves, that they cannot sing can be redeemed by the confidence you show in others' abilities.

3. Teach only songs or harmony lines which you personally have sung in your bath or your bed. If you are uncertain about a song, that will be the first thing your 'trainees' detect.

4. Teach songs only at the appropriate time, which is seldom, if ever, during a church service or even after the organ voluntary.

5. Always introduce a new song with enthusiasm; never with an apology.

---

2   *Innkeepers and Light Sleepers*, pp. 57–60.

6. Use only your voice and hands to teach new tunes.

7. When teaching, sing a bit worse than your best and always use your normal voice.

8. Let the people know about the structure of a tune before you teach it, then teach it in recognisable sections. If the tune does go fairly high, don't petrify people in advance by making a pained expression before the top note. Teach it down a key and later raise the pitch when people are familiar with it.

9. When demonstrating:

    a) sing a verse or a verse and a chorus over first

    b) teach a breath or two lines at a time, whichever is shortest

    c) don't teach a new phrase until the present one is recognisable

    d) sing the tune to 'la' if it looks too big a job to get words and music together at the first go

    e) after the song has been taught, you sing a verse through once, asking people to listen to you and correct, inwardly, their potential mistakes, if any

    f) ask everyone to sing the same verse together (if long verses) or the next verse (if short verses)

    g) always thank and encourage those who are learning

10. When using the song, already learned, in worship, try not to have all the people singing all the time. Either get a soloist to do verse 1, thus refreshing everyone's memory; or get a small group or soloist to sing most of the verses and others join in the chorus, if there is one; or alternate verses between men and women, sides of the church or whatever. People enjoy a song much more when they don't have to sing all of it.

To get people started, you sing the first line to 'la'. To get people singing well, you sit among them and if 'they' are expected to help lead the congregation to sing, think about positioning them not in front of everyone, but behind or among other people. To get the best from new songs, do not teach too many at one time.

I would probably differ from Bell on his point that 'people enjoy a song much more when they don't have to sing all of it'. Bell is a strong advocate of not having everyone singing all the verses. This has certain advantages: it allows long hymns to be sung in full; it adds to the variety of tone and timbre in a piece, a little like the changing of organ register; many of Bell's songs in particular contain dialogue, or the same scene viewed from different perspectives, they therefore suit this approach. However, not all hymns do, and dividing the congregation up too often like this can be irksome and people may feel cheated out of singing a verse they particularly enjoy.

Nevertheless, one can see from these hints how it is presupposed that all the people will be making the effort to sing, regardless of talent. Comments such as 'have confidence in others' abilities', 'sing a little worse than your best' (to avoid intimidation) show Bell's desire to reclaim worship as the activity of the whole people of God, something that Frame[3] acknowledges many contemporary worship environments have taken away, as the congregation listen or simply hum along with the band at the front. His comments regarding how and when to introduce new songs (Rules 4 and 5) are very apt. Often a traditional congregaton will be nervous and insecure about exposing their musical inadequacies; introducing a song apologetically or disrupting the flow of worship by spending several minutes teaching during the service will not put them at ease and could encourage an atmosphere of non-co-operation.

SETTING

The effectiveness of any piece within a service depends on a number of factors including its position in the service, how it is introduced, how it is accompanied, and how many times it is sung. It is vital to point out, therefore, that even the best of material could lose its appeal if handled wrongly. We have all had experiences of favourite songs being 'murdered' because they have been played badly, juxtaposed between entirely unsuitable material, or 'done-to-death'.[4]

The problem is that, in many of our services, little or no thought is given to the function an individual piece plays in the larger whole. Whether one follows a 'hymn sandwich' as is

---

3   See *Contemporary Worship Music*, p. 59.

4   Even a traditionalist like Webster acknowledges the role of setting in determining a hymn's effectiveness. Op. cit., ch. 6.

often the case in traditional Presbyterian worship, or an 'extended worship-time medley' as in many newer churches, continuity and conceptual development are often extremely lacking. While the songs will usually be chosen because they have some relevance thematically, order and relation to the other elements in the service are rarely considered. In one church I attended, for example, the choral anthem was regularly followed by an inane children's ditty. Both may have had their place, but their respective positions meant that the meditative effect of the former was totally lost, and most people cringed through the latter because it was out of context and lacked adequate introduction. If the sermons were as badly organised as the rest of the service, our churches would be emptying a lot faster.

Predictability can easily be avoided, and congregational reflection enhanced by inserting a hymn or short Scripture-song at a point in the service where this would not normally be expected. For example, during the intercessory prayers, after the Benediction, at a particular point in the sermon, or even after the announcement of a piece of particularly good or bad congregational or missionary news. Many hymns which often appear wearisome to sing could be revitalised and a sense of expectation induced through creative introductions involving passages of Scripture, antiphonal calls to worship, and interesting instrumentation. Similarly, the life span of many worship songs could be extended if they were occasionally sung only once, rather than endlessly repeated, or if excerpts from some songs of the last twenty years were woven together giving the worship an interesting sense of breadth. This would help counter the 'cult of the new', where the favourite worship songs of a few years ago are discarded as 'ancient' (to quote a young person from my congregation). Frame makes reference to useful medleys of old and new material,[5] and advocates using a short worship song as a suitable 'Amen' to a more traditional hymn thus achieving 'an edifying blend of the traditional and contemporary'.[6]

---

5   *Contemporary Worship Music*, p. 146.
6   Ibid., p. 138.

The caution towards the new and the tardiness with which contemporary songs have been introduced into the worship services of mainline congregations has led to justifiable frustration on the part of many and has undoubtedly been one of the main motivators behind the formation of new churches. These fellowships have admirably made the encouragement and use of new songs part of their ethos. The Life-Link network of new churches in Ireland, for example, boldly place 'New Songs' alongside their theological distinctives as one of their defining characteristics. The danger, however, is that in encouraging the new, some may develop an attitude whereby the old is too easily discarded, and they thus become a mirror image of the traditionalists who are prejudiced against the contemporary in the cause of safeguarding the old. As young people argue over who is first to possess the new rock CD or first to hear the latest single from the current cult group, the church can be the place for similar competitiveness over who is singing the latest music and who is still stuck on last year's play-list. This primacy given to novelty over worthiness is one area of contemporary culture which needs to be challenged and opposed.

PERFORMANCE

Increased musical literacy and exposure to more music of all varieties in our culture has led to more musicians and a higher expectation of excellence in sound quality. In a good number of new churches, for example, there is usually an impressive group comprising up to a couple of dozen musicians representing the four main orchestral sections, as well as a talented five- or six-piece rock combination, all excellently co-ordinated through a PA system. Yet many mainline churches falter in this area. They have, through their hymn traditions, access to a greater wealth of material, but still we find an over-dominance of organ with perhaps the occasional guitar. There has been a noticeable improvement in the performance of the music, and the availability of musicians, within Evangelicalism, so let us build on this by trying to improve the quality of composition and selection.

The balance here needs to be the recognition that God is more interested in sincerity and in truth than in polished performances. This means that if something worthwhile is performed in a less than perfect manner, the worship can still be acceptable, and it is worth doing again, if appropriate. The equipping of the saints presupposes that the saints will make mistakes! This is not an excuse for shoddiness; unpractised worship bands are not the same as developing musicians who are playing at the limit of their ability but with occasional errors. The former are easy to spot, increase the cringe-factor, and detract from worship, the latter will be understood and their sincerity is often evident. Adequate practice should be seen as a prerequisite, as we seek to give of our best to God.

The key lies in choosing and arranging material to suit the level of competence of the players. In one church in which I was involved we had some keen but very young brass players. The parts I wrote for them rarely consisted of more than three or four notes, but they played these well, and with obvious relish. It was important for them and the congregation that they were there taking part. A professional mindset must not be allowed to degenerate into a crass professionalism whereby competence and excellence become the *only* factors to be considered and we lose sight of wider pastoral and 'body-life' issues. Musicians will need to grow in confidence, and since worship is a community experience, the fact that many different parts of the Body are involved may be in itself something which helps others to worship with thankfulness and joy, regardless of the quality of performance—worship which will naturally be enhanced as confidence grows and the quality improves.

HYMNBOOKS

Recent and rapid technological change has meant that the congregation can be introduced to new material more easily than ever before. The transition from hymnbook to photocopied sheet to overhead projector to computer-controlled projector unit, is certainly indicative of a decreasingly book-orientated culture and a firmer emphasis on the transient. But while new technology facilitates the use of fresh material, it increases the disposability of that material and if used indiscriminately could lead to the disappearance of books altogether and the erosion of a vital link with the heritage of the past.

Disadvantages of Hymnbooks

A more technological approach certainly has several notable advantages over a book:

a) A CD-Rom database is comprehensive. In any book, no matter how good, *popular* hymns will be omitted: no hymnbook is perfect or complete, and every book will have omitted someone's 'favourite'. *New* hymns will be omitted: a hymnbook is out-of-date as soon as (or even before) it is published, with the most contemporary pieces at least three or four years old and some already not staying in wide usage as long as was originally thought. *Good* hymns will be omitted: limiting the choice of material to one book immediately excludes countless valuable hymns, and particularly precludes anything written after the date of compilation.

b) A book is essentially inflexible and cannot be updated easily or successfully.

c) A book can clutter the worship environment. The announcement of numbers and the flicking of pages (and dropping of books) is more likely to disrupt the flow of worship than words immediately projected onto a large screen. Churches who use a more technological method of projecting words speak of how greeters are freed to greet people rather than hand out books and visitors are no longer confused in trying to differentiate between different books or find their way around unfamiliar books. This is particularly true if one is using the combined book of psalms, paraphrases and hymns, common in many Irish and Scottish Presbyterian churches, where the three different numbering and pagination systems cause great confusion to many visitors. This is an interesting example of the 'mote' and the 'log' since Presbyterians are usually among the first to complain about the plethora of unfamiliar prayer-books and hymnbooks when visiting Anglican services.

d) A book tends to inhibit the best singing. With a technological approach, the singing is enhanced by having the worshippers' heads pointed upwards at a screen rather than downwards into a book.

e) By not being limited to a book, home-grown material can be used instantly, and informal contemporary pieces can be used or discarded at will.

f) A CD-Rom database can be updated quickly and necessary amendments to individual hymns can be made easily. For example, linguistic revision, or gender-inclusive terminology can be used to suit the needs of a particular service or congregation. There is also greater flexibility in the selection of verses within a hymn, since a different combination of verses can be used on different occasions without complicated announcement.

g) The technological approach can smooth over the difficult transition many churches experience in changing from one book to another. Many traditionalists dislike singing out of modern books. With this approach these prejudices are undermined since there is no indication of which book is the source. While it could be argued that such people will not sing off a screen, that argument is harder to sustain if the material on the screen is of a sufficient breadth. Complaints will then be focussed on the content of individual pieces rather than on the book, and this is the way it should be.

Advantages of Hymnbooks

Nonetheless, the following advantages to a book cannot be ignored:

a) A book guards an important tradition. First and foremost, the hymnbook selects and protects the best of the past for the church of the present and the near-future. The absence of a well-circulated hymnbook increases the likelihood of many past hymns being lost to today's church.

b) A book is easily accessible, portable and not techno-dependent. To abandon totally the use of a book, leaves one without backup in the eventuality of technological malfunctions or power cuts, and without adequate resources for informal smaller meetings, prayer gatherings and house groups. Smaller churches, especially many rural ones will still be dependent on books for the foreseeable future.

c) The hymnbook is a valuable devotional aid, and many have found it to be a helpful companion to Scripture, especially at times of trouble, crisis, or hospitalisation.

d) A book offers a degree of quality control, and can perform a didactic function as well as a devotional one. There is value in the congregation as a whole having access to a wider repertoire. In the solely technological approach, pieces become too easily discarded and too easily included, and good knowledge of the material is limited to the minister, organist, worship leader, or keeper of the database. It can also be a valuable resource for the education of children. How many of us remember flicking through its pages during dull services and how some of the phrases and words have stuck permanently in our minds? [7]

e) A hymnbook is usually compiled by a group of diverse and knowledgeable musicians, and therefore the selection or exclusion of material is not made at the whim of one person. The absence of a book means that hymns could be lost through acetates and sheets being discarded, or pieces being wiped from a database, in a very haphazard fashion.

---

[7] This point is taken up by D. Ng & V. Thomas in *Children in the Worshiping Community*, Atlanta: John Knox Press, 1981, pp. 39-40.

f) A music book, at least, is still the best trouble-free way to access and survey a lot of material at once. It is easier when choosing praise to flick through a book than scroll down a computer screen (and there are more places one can do it!) It is interesting that even those at the 'cutting edge' of new song-writing still feel it necessary to produce books regularly in order to facilitate the widespread and rapid dissemination of the material.

g) The contents of the hymnbook can give an insight into the theological position(s) of the denomination(s) who commissioned it, and can act as a unifying agent within that denomination. To balance this, however, it is worth noting that the hymnbook is also the one area in which even the most conservative or separatistic churches can be truly ecumenical. Every decent hymnbook will contain offerings from Catholic, High-Anglican, Low-Anglican, Methodist, Calvinist, Anabaptist, Pentecostal and Charismatic sources.

h) The architecture and aesthetics of many churches are not compatible with the best audio-visual options, and a book is still the only realistic option for the short-sighted.

It seems obvious to me that the most sensible way forward is to encourage the use of a database and computer-generated technology where these are feasible, affordable and appropriate, simply because of the flexibility they allow and the breadth of choice they can offer; but to supplement this by having a hymnbook available for individual devotional use, small-group worship, and other situations where screen projection is not feasible or felt to be appropriate. Even if, for pragmatic reasons, the material from the hymnbook is often sung from the screen, the very existence of the hymnal acts as a reminder of the material which is available and should be considered for use in worship, and ensures that the best is not forgotten but continues to exist in a more durable form.

CONCLUSION

'Let me hear you sing, and I will tell you your theology.'

Gordon Fee

The worship of God is our highest calling, involving the giving of our whole selves in obedience to the God who loves us and has redeemed us and called us to be his own. But we are not called in isolation. We are incorporated into the Body of Christ on earth, the community of faith. Therefore, one of our greatest privileges should be the regular meeting with other believers to praise and worship our great God together.

That it should often be characterised by dreariness, tackiness or predictability is an indictment on the church and dishonours the God we seek to serve.

It has been my aim to show some ways in which our sung praise as communities of faith can be improved and injected with greater significance. The previous chapters may be summarised thus.

We need to look back. The Holy Spirit has been active in his church throughout history. An understanding of worship and the role of music did not begin with the Reformation, or charismatic renewal. God has blessed us with the means to read and use the insights and struggles of Watts, Wesley, Cowper, Montgomery, Neale, as well as Idle, Dudley-Smith and Kendrick. To neglect this heritage is to devalue a gift of God and impoverish ourselves spiritually as a result.

We must also look in, examining ourselves and our motivations when we come to worship. Do we come to be entertained, to take from God and others, rather than give of ourselves to God? J. I. Packer, with customary succinctness, gets right to the point here:

> What we need at the present time is not new liturgical forms or formulae, nor new hymns and tunes, but more preparatory 'heart-work' before we use the old ones. There is nothing wrong with new hymns, tunes and worship styles—there may be very good reasons for them—but without

'heart-work' they will not make our worship more fruitful and God-honouring.[1]

This examination is of course a prerequisite for all worshippers, but especially for those whose task it is to lead worship. How prepared are we for this task? How much forethought has gone into it? Has the choice of styles and material represented my personal tastes and prejudices, rather than what may best assist the community in worship? To what extent is my involvement in the leading of worship as a minister, organist, musical director or worship leader an issue of control or a potential source of pride?

We must then look around. We need to look at the culture in which our churches exist and aim to communicate by lyric and music in the language of that culture. Many critics deride the tendency to introduce change just to be trendy and attract people back into the pews. If this is the sole motivation, of course it will be unsuccessful, for the heart and the vision will be lacking. This probably explains why some formerly traditional churches flirt with change, see the negligible effects, then revert back to the old ways, resting forever on the old stand-by excuse 'we tried it and it didn't work'. Nevertheless, the fact remains that many newer churches who have taken seriously their missiological task in this area, and who have radically restructured their worship service, have seen an influx of people whose hearts have been stirred by the worship, and who have been brought face-to-face with God because the praise as well as the preaching has been accessible and relevant.

However, since the culture in which our churches are placed is a heterogeneous, not a homogeneous one, we may have to broaden our missiological focus. There is a common premise that in order to reach today's people we must abandon much of what belongs to a previous era and major on the contemporary musical styles. This is not the complete truth. There is a sizable percentage of our society who will not be attracted in by radical (or even middle-of-the-road) rock, but whose interests and musical tastes lie in a different direction, as the increased interest in Elizabethan and Gregorian music aptly

---

1   J. I. Packer, *A Quest for Godliness*, p. 256.

illustrates. Therefore the best evangelistic strategy may necessitate something a great deal more varied than introducing a drum-kit.

Finally, we should, at all times, look up. The central role of God the Holy Spirit must be kept to the forefront of our minds. One can leave a service of worship thinking: 'it was all good stuff, but there was something missing'. Unless his aid is sought and his presence coveted, all that happens is a charade. The most important thing our Lord Jesus ever taught on the subject of church music was 'Love one another'. If we do not obey him in this respect then even the greatest of musical creations will be but 'a clanging gong or clashing cymbal'.

APPENDIX

Following are two examples of how a wide variety of music could be incorporated into the one service.

Key:

CG	*Common Ground*
EOA	*Enemy of Apathy* (Iona)
GTG	*Glory to God*
HTC	*Hymns for Today's Church*
LFB	*Love From Below* (Iona)
MP	*Mission Praise*
PPPP	*Psalms of Patience, Protest and Praise*, Glasgow: Wild Goose Publications, 1993
RCH	*Revised Church Hymnary*
RPs	*Revised Psalter*
SH	*Spring Harvest*

Option 1: Luke 1:46–56 Mary's Song

General themes—praise, humility, mercy, obedience and sub-mission; God: lover of the poor and weak.

Call to worship

> *Peruvian Gloria* (CG 101)

Opening Praise

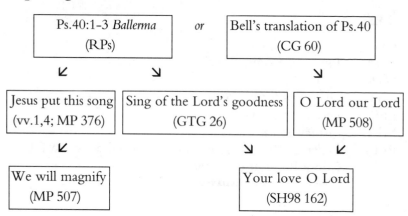

| Ps.40:1–3 *Ballerma* (RPs) | *or* | Bell's translation of Ps.40 (CG 60) |

Jesus put this song (vv.1,4; MP 376) | Sing of the Lord's goodness (GTG 26) | O Lord our Lord (MP 508)

We will magnify (MP 507) | Your love O Lord (SH98 162)

Praise to follow Reading of Scripture

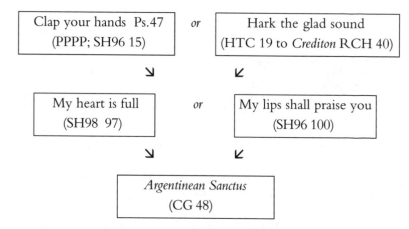

| Clap your hands Ps.47 (PPPP; SH96 15) | *or* | Hark the glad sound (HTC 19 to *Crediton* RCH 40) |

My heart is full (SH98 97) | *or* | My lips shall praise you (SH96 100)

Argentinean Sanctus (CG 48)

Confession Praise

| Purify my Heart (SH98 115) | or | Only By Grace (SH98 107) |

Praise on theme

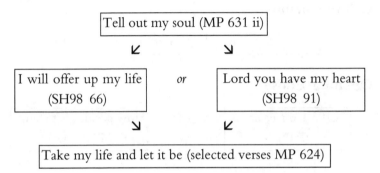

Tell out my soul (MP 631 ii)

I will offer up my life (SH98 66)   or   Lord you have my heart (SH98 91)

Take my life and let it be (selected verses MP 624)

Sung Creed

I Believe (SH96 58)

Suitable Performance music

A Variety of Choral *Magnificats* (depending on standard of singers)
or My Deliverer is coming (R. Mullins)
or My life is in your hands (K. Troccoli)

Intercession Praise

Mayenziwe ('Your will be done' CG 84)

Responsive/Closing Praise

The trumpets sound (MP 667)

Amen

Amen siyakudumisa (CG 7)

<u>Option 2: Luke 4:31–44 Jesus the Healer</u>

General themes—God: his power and authority; healing, trust in God, victory, spiritual warfare

Call to worship

> Come all you people (CG 18)

Opening Praise

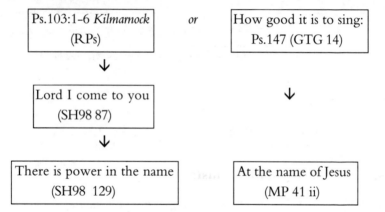

| Ps.103:1–6 *Kilmarnock* (RPs) | *or* | How good it is to sing: Ps.147 (GTG 14) |

↓

| Lord I come to you (SH98 87) | | ↓ |

↓

| There is power in the name (SH98 129) | | At the name of Jesus (MP 41 ii) |

Praise to follow Reading of Scripture

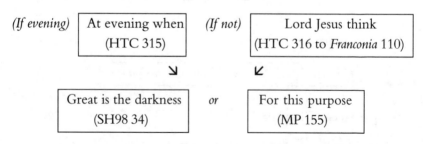

(If evening) | At evening when (HTC 315) | *(If not)* | Lord Jesus think (HTC 316 to *Franconia* 110) |

↘ ↙

| Great is the darkness (SH98 34) | *or* | For this purpose (MP 155) |

Confession Praise

| Rock of ages (MP 582 v.3) | *or* | Who can sound (MP 766 v.5) | *or* | God be merciful to me (GTG 43) |

Praise on theme

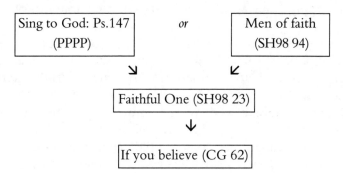

| Sing to God: Ps.147 (PPPP) | *or* | Men of faith (SH98 94) |

Faithful One (SH98 23)

If you believe (CG 62)

Intercession Praise

| O Lord hear my prayer) (CG 94) | *or* | We will lay our burdens down (LFB 82) |

Sung Creed

We Believe (MP 720)

Suitable Performance music

Jairus's Daughter—*She Moves Through the Fair* (EOA 18)
or   The Gentle Healer (Michael Card)
or   Ball and chain (S. Ashton)
or   Broken Things (Julie Millar)
or   Everybody Hurts (REM)

Responsive/Closing Praise

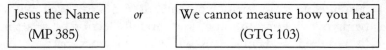

| Jesus the Name (MP 385) | *or* | We cannot measure how you heal (GTG 103) |

I recognise that different churches and denominations will have different approaches to the ordering of the contents of a worship service. This appendix is designed simply to demonstrate what types of music can be employed around the basic components of call to worship, Scripture reading, confession, intercession, response to the Word, and Benediction.

Alternatives are placed on the same line, with arrows indicating which pieces would flow well together. Sometimes these are interchangeable. For example, after the reading of Scripture under Option 1, 'My heart is full' could easily follow either 'Clap your hands' or 'Hark the Glad sound'.

Creativity will be required in how some of the pieces are presented. *Ballerma*, for example (Option 1), is probably best sung unaccompanied. This can add considerable feeling to what can become a dreary tune, and also allow either of the three lively alternatives on the next line to start with a 'bang' of full accompaniment. In option 2, I recognise that *Franconia*, is not the most exciting of tunes, but there is a total dearth of interesting Short Metre tunes, and the words are too good to lose. Again, unaccompanied singing may help.

Older psalm versions which have lost their meaning through being sung in isolation and through too many verses being accompanied by a dominant organ, could be reinvested with meaning if shorter fragments of them were used in a variety of ways at different parts of the service.

Similarly, appropriate individual verses of well-known hymns can be used to accompany intercessions or (as option 2 shows) confessions. Here 'God be merciful to me' set to the plaintive Welsh tune *Aberystwyth*, should be broken up with perhaps one verse before, one during, and one after the prayers.

While this may seem to be a lot more singing than is currently used in many churches, it can flow well without being overly long. In some cases careful selection of verses may be required, and musicians will have to work hard at good 'bridges' between songs, which are strong but not long.